A Question of Conscience

First published in 2013

by Londubh Books

18 Casimir Avenue, Harold's Cross, Dublin 6w, Ireland

www.londubh.ie

Reprinted 2013

3 5 4 2

Origination by Londubh Books; cover by bluett; cover photograph by Jaketerina Saveljeva

Printed by ScandBook AB Falun, Sweden

ISBN: 978-1-907535-30-7

A Question of Conscience

Tony Flannery

LONDUBH BOOKS

This book is dedicated to all those who love the Catholic Church and for this reason are committed to reform and renewal according to the teachings of the Second Vatican Council.

Contents

Foreword by Mary McAleese

In his speech at the opening of the Second Vatican Council on 11 October 1962, Pope John XXIII said:

'Today, however, Christ's Bride prefers the balm of mercy to the arm of severity. She believes that present needs are best served by explaining more fully the purport of her doctrines, rather than by publishing condemnations...Everywhere, through her children, she extends the frontiers of Christian love, the most powerful means of eradicating the seeds of discord, the most effective means of promoting concord, peace with justice, and universal brotherhood.

'...with the opening of this Council a new day is dawning on the Church, bathing her in radiant splendour. It is yet the dawn, but the sun in its rising has already set our hearts aglow.'

Tony Flannery's heart was set aglow with a passion for the gospel and for the Church and two years after that famous opening day, at the age of seventeen, he joined the Redemptorist order, dedicating his life to the priesthood and to the people of God. He will soon celebrate the fortieth anniversary of his ordination to the priesthood and what a priesthood it has been: a deeply empathetic and listening pastor, a preacher and teacher par excellence, a loving but scrupulously faithful critic of his fallible and at times failing Church, a man of faith and courage, unafraid to be a voice of contradiction, to turn his back on the crowd and lead in the direction he conscientiously believes the Lord is calling.

On 24 April 2013, at a Mass in Casa Santa Marta in Rome, Pope Francis said:

'The Church is in a love story...The Church is not a bureaucratic organisation, but a love story...the Church is not just any other organisation, she is Mother...[not] a domestic administrator, no, the Church is Mother.'

The imagery is beautiful and heartening, just as the words of Pope John were, over fifty years ago. But I ask myself what mother treats a son as Tony Flannery has been treated?

Tony tells the story of his relationship with that mother in the pages that follow. I will leave the reader to judge for him or herself whether those reassuring Papal words have been honoured as they should have been.

Introduction

Eighteen months ago I became aware that three of the Vatican congregations, the bodies in Rome that make up the government of the Catholic Church, had met and talked about me: the Congregation for the Doctrine of the Faith; the Congregation for the Clergy; and the Congregation for the Institutes of Consecrated Life and Societies of Apostolic Life, usually known as the Congregation for Religious. Up until that time, it would never have occurred to me that anyone in these congregations would bother about me, even though priests like me knew there were people in the Irish Church who were keeping them well informed.

Apparently there was concern about my writings in *Reality*, an Irish religious magazine. At least this is what I was told. The upshot of these discussions was that the Congregation for the Doctrine of the Faith (CDF) made accusations, passed judgement and decreed the penalties that were to be imposed, before I was even aware that anything was happening. So obviously I was on some Vatican list before I even knew about it.

For a whole year I attempted to deal with the concerns of the CDF, a task made difficult by the refusal of the Vatican to deal directly with me. All communications came through the superior general of my order, the Redemptorists, and the documents that originated in the Vatican were simply typed A4 pages, with no form of identification.

In January 2013, having submitted two different statements of my faith that were rejected by the CDF, I found myself in a situation where I could do no more. It seemed to me that we had reached the end of the road. I was forbidden to minister as a priest and the conditions of returning to ministry were such that I could not comply with them without compromising my own integrity. At this point I decided to go public about the whole process. Up to then I had remained silent and observed the strictures of secrecy imposed by the Church authorities as best I could, without doing too much damage to my own mental and emotional state.

My decision to go public was made slowly and carefully and for a very specific reason. Since I had given up hope of being allowed to minister as a priest again I believed that the best way I could continue to serve the Church was by bringing into the light of day to the best of my ability the arcane and unjust processes that are the *modus operandi* of the CDF. Some months ago, when I described the action being taken against me to members of the legal team that works for the Association of Catholic Priests, they were amazed that such a form of 'justice' could still be in operation in the 21st century.

This book, a further attempt to bring to light the workings of the CDF, is in many ways a simple story, simply told. While it is my personal story it is not really about me. It is about the Vatican and how its constituent bodies deal with people who challenge any of their views, who question official Church positions. Any questions raised about the exercise of Church authority, the ministry, or the Church's teaching on sexuality are closely scrutinised and dissent is simply not tolerated.

When people discuss a row, they often remark that the immediate cause of the quarrel is not the real cause – this lies buried back in some unfinished business, some unresolved issue. One of the difficulties I am currently experiencing is that I am not at all sure whether the CDF's stated concerns are its real ones. If they were, it should surely have been possible to discuss the situation with me directly and sort it out without too much difficulty. It seems significant that the CDF did not express disquiet about my writings until after the founding and rapid development of the Association of Catholic Priests.

I acknowledge the great support I got from many people during the past eighteen months. I wish to mention especially my family and close friends, whose encouragement and assistance were indispensable. Many of my colleagues in the Redemptorists have been enormously supportive and I am very grateful to them, while I accept that some of the older members of the order have found it difficult to understand that a fellow Redemptorist would be in public conflict with the leadership of the Church. My co-leaders in the ACP have been rock-solid all the way and some have put their own necks on the line to support me.

During these past difficult months I have received numerous messages of support from people all over the world, something that has been inspirational and also very humbling. I know that to some extent I have become a voice for people who are on the fringes of the Church, people who care about the Church and who are experiencing sadness at its current decline. I believe that it is important that I continue to witness to the truths that many of us prize, as a means of honouring the hopes and aspirations of these members of the faithful. This belief has influenced my decisions since this process began.

Special thanks to Terry Prone of the Communications Clinic for her generous help and expertise.

Finally, I want to thank my publisher, Jo O'Donoghue, for her advice, support and skilful and tireless editing.

Tony Flannery
June 2013

1

A Changing Church

How did I get to where I am now, at sixty-six years of age?

I was ordained in 1974 along with four others in the Redemptorist Congregation in Ireland. One has died, the rest of us are still in the priesthood. Considering the time at which we were ordained it is probably surprising that none of us has left, at least not yet!

The Redemptorists are a religious congregation founded by Alphonsus Liguori in southern Italy in 1732. The main purpose of the founder and his immediate followers was to be a body of men who would devote their lives to 'preaching the word of God to the poor'. The congregation came to Ireland in the middle of the 19th century and the main way in which the members worked out their charism in the Irish Church was by being travelling preachers, conducting special events (missions, novenas, retreats) with the aim of renewing and revitalising the faith of the communities to which they were invited.

In Ireland Redemptorists traditionally had a reputation for hard-line moralistic preaching and were popularly known as the 'hellfire' or 'fire and brimstone' preachers. They tended to be strong and colourful and for that reason they made a considerable impact in those early years, when people were poor and uneducated. In many instances, the parish mission was viewed as a form of entertainment, bringing drama into the lives of the parishioners. Stories of the missions preached by Redemptorists figure in the literature of the first half of the twentieth century, most notably in the work of Patrick Kavanagh. There is a very graphic and dramatic sermon scene in James Joyce's *A Portrait of the Artist as a Young Man*, which is often attributed to a Redemptorist but was actually preached by a Jesuit.

For their first century in Ireland the life of Redemptorists followed a closely-defined pattern of work and message. The topics for their sermons at missions and retreats were set and there were even manuals with the text of sermons. Preachers were allowed some flexibility in the way they presented sermons, by introducing their own stories and examples, but they had to stick closely to the message. Some of them became famous for what was termed 'putting the fear of God into people'. The official text in the *Blue Book* for the opening sermon of a Redemptorist mission begins:

'"It has been granted unto man but once to die and after death the judgment." My dear brethren in Jesus Christ. As I gaze down tonight at your upturned faces I know not your names or your ages; of your station in life I am also ignorant. I know not if you be rich or poor, strong or weak. But there is one truth I know about each and every one of you, one great, eternal truth; that each and every one of you will one day die.'

It is hard for us now fully to comprehend the impact of this type of sermon. For one thing it was delivered without the aid of a microphone, so the preacher's voice needed to be loud and strong and dominating to fill a large church. The priest was on a pulpit, well above the people and dressed in a black cassock or habit, as we Redemptorists call our attire. He had a biretta on his head and a large crucifix hanging from his neck. The people were largely uneducated and the power of the Catholic Church at the time was enormous.

One particular Redemptorist carried on a long campaign against the manufacture of poitín (a potent illegal spirit). There is no doubt that there was a real problem with the consumption of this spirit but his method of trying to eradicate it was colourful, to say the least. The ceremony of burning the poitín stills in the village green on the closing evening of the mission is still talked about along the western seaboard of Ireland.

The Redemptorist preachers of this time lived a very strict life in their monasteries. The ideal that was put before them was to be 'Carthusians at home and apostles abroad'. (The Carthusians are an order of contemplative religious.) I suspect that part of the reason their preaching was often severe and condemnatory was the harshness of their own lives. There were very few concessions to the humanity of the person. The spirituality of the time promoted a complete denial of oneself and submission to the will of the superior as the will of God.

This was the tradition my generation of Redemptorists inherited. We had grown up and gone to college in the 1960s, when the spirit of revolution and protest was in the air, and we belonged to a Church that was full of excitement about the new vision that had come from the Second Vatican Council. I still find it extraordinary to think that in a short period during my early days in the Redemptorists the fundamental theme of our preaching underwent such a major shift. Our focus changed from death and eternity to the famous saying of St Irenaeus: 'The glory of God is the human person fully alive,' a quotation used recently, I was pleased to see, by Pope Francis.

In my later student days and during the early years of my priesthood, a great wave of renewal swept through the Redemptorists. In a very short space of time we transformed ourselves from being one of the most traditional and moralistic orders to being in the forefront of change and renewal in the Irish Church. This was dramatic and to be young in this atmosphere was exciting.

I don't think anyone has yet written accurately about why this enormous change happened to us but I give most of the credit to two individuals who assumed positions of authority in those years. A young man called Jim McGrath, working on the mission in Brazil, was unexpectedly elected Irish provincial (national leader) of the Redemptorists in 1969. Ironically for such a dynamic leader, he was a compromise candidate. Jim was tall and rangy and it was accepted by all that it would be the height of foolishness to approach him before he had his first cup of coffee in the morning. He also loved to play golf, an activity that was generally frowned on by the older men at the time as not being appropriate activity for religious. I am grateful to him for that legacy, among many others. He was a man with a great breadth of vision and he immediately began to give the younger generation of priests their head, encouraging them to carve out a new message for that new era in the Church.

The second man was Stan Mellett, who had returned from working in India and was appointed superior of our main foundation in Ireland, the house in Limerick. Stan was from Kilfenora, County Clare, and he too realised that change was needed and had the courage to take the necessary risks. In the 1970s the Limerick monastery became the centre of the order's renewal. I was very lucky to have spent two years there, from 1971-3, while still a student. I was on the verge of leaving the congregation at that stage but those years in Limerick filled me with excitement and a sense of the great possibilities that were opening up for the Church after the Second Vatican Council. It was in that era and with that mindset that I decided I would accept ordination to the priesthood.

It is hard to think oneself back into an earlier period in life. What level of awareness did I have at that stage? What did I really think about the commitment to celibacy and its long-term implications? Of course I had no idea that I would live to see what I am now experiencing in the Church. My companions and I, in the innocence and naïvité of youth, fully believed that the old ways were dead and gone and that a bright new era had dawned.

After ordination I was sent straight in to work, with all the exhilaration this involved. Preaching came easily to me and I discovered that I came alive in a way that I had never before experienced when I stood in front of a churchful of people. Even at my first Mass in a little church in Killimordaly in County Galway I spoke without a script and despite some initial nervousness, I quickly relaxed and communicated freely and easily with the people.

I learned a great deal in those early years from working with my colleagues on the Redemptorist mission teams. They believed firmly that we should always be willing to listen to the people before we stood up to preach, so we spent much of our time visiting people in their homes and holding small discussion groups in their neighbourhoods. We could no longer do as our precursors in the Redemptorists had done in the pulpit: present Church teaching as something to be imposed in a rigid and unbending way. Instead as preachers we tried to present the message of Christ in a way and in a language that spoke to life as our audience lived it. To this day I am extremely grateful to my more experienced colleagues who taught me this crucial lesson at such an early stage. It remains a dominant factor in my thinking about priestly ministry. This is not to say that my preaching was always perfect. Looking back, I feel a degree of embarrassment that I expounded on marriage and family and even on sexuality. What is surprising is that I can only ever remember one occasion on which a woman confronted me and told me that I did not, could not, know what I was talking about.

Hearing confessions was then a big part of our work as Redemptorists. We spent many hours in small, airless, confession boxes, while people came in and out, often sharing with us the deepest and most intimate parts of their lives. To be fair to us, we generally managed to convey to people that we were open and ready to listen without passing judgement. The influence of two of our moral theologians of the time, Sean O'Riordan and Gerry Crotty, contributed greatly to this. We learned not only to listen but, even more importantly, that people generally had the ability to make the best decisions for their own lives, if they got some help and encouragement. Sitting and listening to them tease out the issues in the light of their faith brought home strongly to us that a great many of them were intelligent and educated and well able to make their own decisions.

The experience of listening to people was invaluable for keeping us in touch with the reality of their lives and brought home to us that Irish Catholics were increasingly thinking for themselves, rapidly emerging from the era when the Church was dominant and they did as they were told. This was the type of environment in which we were glad to work. We were imbued with the teaching of the Second Vatican Council, which states clearly that human beings are bound to follow their conscience.

When I began hearing confessions the Church's teaching on contraception was constantly mentioned by young married women. (Men seldom mentioned it!) This was less than a decade after the publication of *Humanae Vitae* (1968), a document that brought great disappointment to many Catholics. Clearly it was a serious problem for the women who raised it. Again, looking back, I can see that this situation was somewhat absurd. Here was I, a young priest who had lived quite a sheltered life and knew nothing about the real stresses and strains of marriage, trying to advise a young woman on the most intimate area of her relationship, in a dark confession box where all you could see of the person to whom you were talking was a shadowy outline.

But helping people to deal with this was a great training ground. We Redemptorists knew that just repeating the official line of *Humanae Vitae* was of no help. Instead we tried to help these women to make their own conscientious decisions, taking into consideration the different aspects of their lives and in particular the type of relationship they had with their husbands. It was very difficult to do this in the context of the confession box: after you had spent anything up to three hours cooped up in there, going over the same ground many times, you were usually exhausted. Sometimes we had the inclination to make the decision for them but we knew this was no good. The days of telling people what to do were gone and we knew that if people could make this decision for themselves it would stand to them for their lives.

During those years priests and people alike learned a lot about how to form their conscience and make mature decisions about various areas in their lives. As priests, we learned more from people than they learned from us as we were all gradually freed from an oppressive obedience. The power of the official Church to control its members was drastically weakened: sadly, it gradually lost not only the power to control but the power to influence. Once people decided that Church teaching on the use of artificial birth control within marriage did not make sense, they quickly lost faith in the Church's capacity to have anything significant to say on human sexuality.

The present Papal Nuncio to Ireland, Archbishop Charles John Brown, described the ideal priest as one who works away quietly, 'without publicity or fanfare'. I was that type of priest for a good part of my life. I lived in a Redemptorist monastery and went out with my suitcase packed to preach parish missions and novenas. It was work I enjoyed. I wasn't afraid of speaking in public. I never suffered very much from nerves, except for a short period in my early priestly life when I had something of a mini-breakdown, brought on by overwork and the fact that I was using my work as a way of coping with my own insecurities. That period taught me a lot about myself and my ministry and thankfully, within a year, I was back in full swing but with a bit more detachment and a healthier sense of balance in my life.

It was enjoyable and privileged work and especially in the early years I had great energy for it. I tried to share the pain of parents who had discovered that their son or daughter was gay, or who were torn between what the Church said on this issue and their own love for their child. I heard from people in later life – widows, widowers, single people – who had found a companion but who struggled with guilt over the physical expression of their affection.

I also spent a good part of each year conducting school retreats, the hardest work of all. A team of us would spend anything up to a week in a school, taking each class for a day's retreat in the classroom. As the retreat took place within the context of school, we were dependent on the atmosphere that prevailed in that particular school, so some of these retreats were marvellous, while others were very difficult. They gave us a first-hand insight into the attitudes, values and problems of the young generation.

I could see very clearly how the Church was losing touch with young people, how its language and style of communication were no longer getting through to them. As a result many young people did not understand or appreciate fundamental Christian teaching on such issues as life, love and relationships. I have already referred to the Church's lack of influence in these areas after the publication of *Humanae Vitae* and it was in working with young people that this lack became most obvious. The tendency of the Church was to get caught up in particular issues and to present them in such an extreme and inflexible way that they no longer made sense to the young. This was very frustrating for those of us who were trying to give the Church a human face. More often than not when we stood in front of a group of young people we had to overcome their very negative preconceived ideas about priests and religious before we could begin to make progress. Often this took up most of the available time.

Many a time I came home from a day in a school wondering what was the point of it all, although, every now and again, a group would show an ability to grapple with the deeper issues of life and faith that was exhilarating. Throughout those years it was all too obvious that we were mostly failing in our efforts to pass on the faith to the new generation.

2

The Power of the Pen

For about twenty years of my life as a priest I worked hard, as the Papal Nuncio advised, 'without publicity or fanfare'. But all sorts of questions were presenting themselves to me. I loved the work, I loved preaching the Gospel and had no doubt that it was a powerful and necessary message for our time. So I always stood at the ambo, or mounted the pulpit in a church, with complete conviction that I had something to say, as long as I tried to present the message of Jesus as best I could. I have never doubted that He really is 'the Word that gives life' but I increasingly asked myself whether the institutional Church was proving an obstacle to conveying the message rather than a help.

I remember that early morning in September 1979 in Ballybrit, on the outskirts of Galway, when the new pope, John Paul II, charmed the young people of Ireland. I was one of a large group of priests sitting near the altar and was initially caught up in the excitement of the young people and the obvious dramatic power of this man from Poland. But the more I listened to what he had to say, the more my excitement waned. As the pope walked off the altar at the end of the ceremony he passed very close to where I was standing. I was in a perfect position to shake his hand or get his blessing. But there was an older priest pressing in behind me, who was clearly very anxious to make some contact with the pope, and I happily stood aside for him. It was partly a gesture to accommodate the wishes of the older man but I was also aware that within myself I was not particularly anxious to greet the pope.

I came away from that gathering with a heavy heart, although I was not too sure why I felt that way. Looking back now I can see that I sensed at some level that under this pope we were heading into a period of retrenchment, that the hopes and dreams we had for the Church were going to be dashed. The following day the Pope addressed seminarians in Maynooth. Michael Harding has written fairly scathingly about that event and I clearly recall a telephone conversation I had with one of my fellow priests on the subject. He said that when he heard the Pope's address to the trainee priests on the radio, he felt like switching off the transistor and hurtling it against the wall – a sure case of shooting the messenger! I have always had a tendency, rightly or wrongly, to study people's faces, especially when I meet strangers. I know now that what I saw in the pope's face that day was a hardness, a tightness around the mouth and the eyes, that foreshadowed the authoritarianism, the wagging of the finger and the laying down of the law that were to characterise his reign. I never warmed to him after that day.

It was many years before I decided that the Nuncio's ideal priest was not adequate for the times we lived in: that there was too much that was dysfunctional about the Church and Vatican that needed to be voiced. In the early 1990s, I began to write articles and speak publicly on very carefully chosen occasions about the problems in the Church. I had no sense then where this would lead twenty years later.

I was at this time the superior of our monastery in Limerick. For us, the two highlights of the liturgical year were Midnight Mass at Christmas and Easter Sunday morning and as superior I had the privilege of preaching on these occasions. They were times when people came to church who would not normally do so, particularly those of the younger generation. I decided to use the occasions to address my audience and speak to them openly about the difficulties in the Church. I discussed issues such as the use of authority within the Church, the problems around the appointment of bishops, the difficulties that were beginning to develop around priesthood and various aspects of the sexual teaching of the Church.

The people of Limerick knew me and were not surprised to hear these types of talks but it wasn't too long until the media began to pick up on them. I remember my first experience of dealing with the media when a journalist from a national newspaper rang to ask for comments on the talk I had given on a particular occasion – on which subject I cannot remember. He was friendly and encouraging on the phone, so I ended up speaking more freely to him than was wise. The following day I was taken aback by the version of the story that was presented, under a very sensational headline. This was the first of many lessons I was to learn about dealing with the media and even now, twenty years later, I need constantly to remind myself that the agenda of broadcasters or journalists is different from mine.

The first article I had published was in the Irish religious magazine, *The Furrow*. I had just got a word processor, which meant that I could easily correct my typing mistakes. At last I began to have enough confidence to put my many questions and concerns about the state of the faith and the Church into print. When I finished my term as superior of the monastery I was due a sabbatical. Rather than going off to some institute to study, as was the norm, I decided that I would write a book. (My other ambition for that year was to get my golf handicap down to single figures, which I achieved before the book was published!) I moved out of the monastery and into my old family home, which had been empty since the death of our parents but which my siblings and I kept as a holiday home, or maybe a refuge for those of us in religious life. I lived there for a year on my own. After a lifetime in a religious community it took me a while to settle into the rhythms of cooking, cleaning and looking after a house and to get used to the loneliness of not having anyone else around. But once I got used to it I loved the freedom and the quiet of those days.

Writing has been a big part of my life ever since. I have heard other writers say that it is essential to discipline oneself to spend a set period of time writing each day. This has never been the way it works for me. When I am in the mood and the words are coming easily I can make a lot of progress. At other times every sentence is a torture and my writing is flat and dead on the page. Whenever possible, I try to wait for the right time to sit at the computer and begin to write.

My first book concerned the state of religious life as I had experienced it. I began writing in October and the book was published the following April. Anybody who has ever written a book will know the excitement, first of getting a publisher, then of holding the finished product in your hand, with your name writ large on the cover. The title of this first book was *The Death of Religious Life?* (I learned quickly that it is not a good idea to have a title with a question mark at the end, because this piece of punctuation is quickly ignored and what began as a question is generally read as a statement.) Its main thesis was that the style of religious life, known as 'apostolic', that was lived by most congregations of men and women, including my own, was in terminal decline. I argued that, rather than wasting our effort and energy trying to sustain something that had no future, we should accept the reality and prepare for as clean and painless a demise as possible. I believed that this style of religious life, most elements of which dated from the 18th and 19th centuries, had made a great contribution but that it was no longer fulfilling an essential need. I argued that a few orders might manage to reinvent themselves and find a new reason for existence but that most would not be able to do so and would inevitably die.

A good illustration of this was the large number of religious orders that were founded in the 19th century to educate the children of the poorer classes – and indeed also of the upper classes. They did great work but gradually as the twentieth century progressed this work was taken over by the state and they became redundant. It now appears that many of these orders have failed to reinvent themselves and are in terminal decline.

The Death of Religious Life? was not well received by many of my own colleagues in religious life, something that did not surprise me. I knew I was making life harder for the person appointed to promote vocations by saying that we should not take any more recruits because we had no long-term future. Unfortunately, the reality of the decline we are living through now, sixteen years later, is far greater than I visualised then.

My next book, *From the Inside*, published in 1999, was a personal account of my life as a priest, which explored the development of my thinking during my twenty-five years in religion. It sold very well and, unusually for a book with a religious subject, remained on the Irish bestseller list for about four months, placing me in the public eye much more than heretofore. There were a number of controversial parts but it did not draw the ire of the Vatican; nor did a book I wrote a couple of years later, entitled *Keeping the Faith*. During these years I also wrote a regular monthly column for the Redemptorist publication *Reality*.

3

The Association of Catholic Priests

The scandal of clerical sex abuse really came to prominence in the Irish Church when the story of Brendan Smyth, a Norbertine priest who was a serial paedophile, was revealed. It was clear that this man had abused a great number of children over many years and that there had been a terrible failure by both Church and state authorities to deal with him. His case became a *cause célèbre* in Ireland, bringing about the collapse of the government at the end of 1994.

I remember that two of my colleagues and I were conducting a mission in a Cork city parish while the Brendan Smyth affair was being played out on the national airwaves. While this was going on it was very difficult to go out each evening to face the people. We began to feel for the first time a sense of shame about being in an official position in the Church, with the realisation that people were beginning to look at us priests in a new, less favourable light, even with some suspicion. We didn't realise that this was just the beginning and that a great many other horrific stories would be revealed over the next decades that would change the face of the priesthood and of the Catholic Church in Ireland and around the world.

From this point on the fall-off in church attendance began to accelerate rapidly and life became more difficult for priests. The great dream of a new and vibrant Church, which had inspired me and most of my contemporaries to become priests, had turned into a nightmare. Instead of a Church confident in itself and its message and open to the world, we found ourselves in an institution that was falling apart. Unspeakable crimes were being revealed and the authorities seemed incapable of dealing with the situation. At parish level, where priests were well known and liked by the people, there wasn't too much negative reaction. But nationally, due to constant media exposure, the words 'priest' and 'paedophile' increasingly became associated. Though I never personally experienced any unpleasantness or abuse from people in public, I heard many stories of other priests enduring fairly awful verbal assaults.

During these years we priests struggled with a mixture of emotions. There was a sense of shame and horror at what some of our colleagues had done, as well as anger at bishops and religious superiors for their failure to act promptly and decisively. We felt a sense of utter frustration with the Vatican, because Church leaders consistently refused to look at the deeper questions raised by this issue. For instance, we knew that child sexual abuse was a problem right across society but it was clear that the incidence of abuse was at least as high among priests and religious as among the total population. This was a big disappointment, considering the values by which we priests and religious were supposed to live. We wanted the question of clerical celibacy to be examined, as well as what was called 'the culture of clericalism'. But the Vatican persisted in looking outside the clerical system and indeed outside the Church for the causes of the problem, blaming things like the level of moral values in society generally, the permissiveness of the 1960s and lack of prayer in the lives of priests. They blocked any real debate about the deeper issues, in my view doing no more than papering over the cracks.

As well as being shocked by the mishandling of clerical sexual abuse, I was more and more disappointed by the increasing centralisation of the power structure of the Church. The Vatican is composed of a series of 'congregations' that deal with different aspects of the government of the Church, a structure somewhat similar to the various branches of the civil service that provide the essential mechanism of government in democratic states. During the later years of the papacy of Pope John Paul II and again during that of Benedict XVI, the Congregation for the Doctrine of the Faith (CDF) assumed more and more control over the whole Church and instead of being a servant of the decision makers, actually became a decision maker itself. It was an unhealthy development. The hopes arising from the Second Vatican Council, of a new style of governance based on collegiality, were trampled upon; instead we seemed to be heading back to a 19th-century model of Church. Meanwhile, in Ireland we had bishops who, while good and sincere in themselves, seemed to possess no real leadership ability, never venturing in public an opinion that in any way challenged the *diktat* of Rome.

A happy coincidence brought myself and a Columban priest, Sean McDonagh, together one evening in May 2010. Sean worked in many parts of the developing world and is noted for his work on ecology, expressed in the numerous books and articles he has written on the damage being done to our environment. He has been for many years in the forefront of the call for a change of lifestyle and of government policy, highlighting in particular the way in which the economic decisions of developed nations can have catastrophic consequences for the developing world. He is a man of extraordinary breadth and depth of knowledge. He was then back home in Ireland and our conversation ranged over the problems in the Irish Church, especially in the priesthood. We decided that we would invite a few priests to meet us to discuss the situation. As I thought over the next few days of who I might invite to that meeting I had no doubt who was at the top of my list. Brendan Hoban is a priest of the small diocese of Killala, in the north-west of Ireland. In my experience diocesan priests tend to be more cautious than those in religious communities but Brendan has always been the exception to this. With his clarity of thought, his courage and his exceptional skill with words, he has been one of the most significant voices for change and renewal in the Irish Church for the past thirty years, so I was delighted when he agreed to join us for a discussion.

In all, eight of us, including two of my own Redemptorist colleagues, came together in Athlone in June 2010, to discuss the possibility of setting up some type of organisation to speak for priests. There had been a priests' organisation in Ireland, known as the National Conference of Priests, for many years but it had been set up by the bishops and it was carefully monitored and controlled. As a consequence priests did not have much interest in it. It was seen as a fairly ineffective body and eventually it died through lack of interest. We believed that there was great need for an association to give us a voice. It was agreed at the initial meeting that three of us, Sean, Brendan and I, would explore the possibility of setting up some kind of representative body. Three months later, three hundred priests came together and the Association of Catholic Priests was launched, with the three of us in a joint leadership role. (P.J. Madden later became the fourth member of the leadership team.)

We decided at the very beginning that we would not try to represent all priests in Ireland because of the great variety of opinions and attitudes among them. Instead we drew up a list of aims and objectives – primarily the renewal of the Church in line with the teachings of the Second Vatican Council and achieving a voice for priests – and invited those who shared these aims to join the association. We were surprised at the enthusiasm of the initial response: it was clear that this was an idea whose time had come. We learned very quickly that many priests felt exposed and isolated and no longer had confidence in Church authorities to stand by them if they got into any sort of trouble.

The second surprise was that we quickly had requests for help from priests against whom allegations of various types had been made, mostly to do with child sexual abuse. These men had become the new 'outcasts'. Although we were initially very ambivalent about this we came around to thinking that, even when priests had done wrong, as followers of Christ we needed to show compassion to the sinner and provide some type of support for them, as they told us they were getting little or no support from their bishops, or often, indeed, from religious superiors.

At this point we had a really lucky break. Through some contacts we managed to get in touch with a team of legal people, including solicitor Robert Dore, who agreed to work *pro bono* for us to help and support priests. We have worked closely with Robert for more than two years and he has put an incalculable amount of time and effort into helping our members. What I find most impressive about him is his compassion: no matter what the situation of the priests and no matter what they have done, he is invariably sympathetic and courteous and helps them in every way he can.

The legal component of the association got a big boost early on when the team successfully defended a priest who had been seriously defamed in an RTÉ television documentary. The other development that drew new members to us was the action of the Vatican in censoring five of our members in various ways.

At the time of writing, after three years in existence, the Association of Catholic Priests has a membership of well over a thousand, more than we ever dreamed possible, although it would be foolish to think that all these priests are equally committed to the reform of the Church, as outlined in our aims and objectives. We did our best to postpone the introduction of the new missal in 2011 and we have also agitated about the problems of ministry: the fact that in twenty years time there will be very few priests to celebrate the Eucharist for the faithful. Although providing the Eucharist is one of the most important functions of Church authorities, we find it hard to get any bishop to make a public statement on this issue.

Priests' organisations have sprung up in many countries around the world and we are liaising with one another, which makes our influence more significant. Sometimes I believe that this development is the work of the Holy Spirit who breathes where he/she will. It has captured the imagination of many Catholics who want a different model of Church.

Just when I and my colleagues felt we could begin again to dream of a renewed Church, to paraphrase the song from *Les Misérables*, life killed the dream.

4

The Congregation for the Doctrine of the Faith

I never expected to have to deal with the Congregation for the Doctrine of the Faith. I had read about them and their history under various guises, including the Holy Office and the Inquisition. But I had never been particularly interested in the inner workings of the Curia, which are often a source of clerical gossip, although I occasionally enjoyed hearing the latest rumour from St Peter's Square, when some of my colleagues from Rome were visiting Ireland or when I was there on business. I think that the further one is positioned from the centre of authority the less interest one has in the political manoeuvres that mark all institutions, including the Catholic Church.

Like many priests, what gave me energy and renewed whatever faith I have was working with ordinary believers in the parishes. Before the Second Vatican Council the general government of my congregation, the Redemptorists, had enormous power and Rome appointed all the superiors. But after the Council there were big changes, so that all major decisions were made at national level and members of the general government were little more than figureheads to us priests. About twenty years ago I was a member of one of the secretariats of the general government for a few years, which entailed attending some meetings at our headquarters in Rome. That was about the limit of my experience of the world of Redemptorist general government, so when I got a phone call to tell me that the Congregation for the Doctrine of the Faith had set their sights on me it was a shock, a bolt from the blue.

One of the big difficulties of dealing with Catholic Church authorities is the enormous emphasis they put on secrecy as an essential component of the whole exercise. While secrecy, or discretion, as I would prefer to call it, is vital in significant areas of our lives, the Vatican's emphasis on it from the beginning of this saga was extraordinary. I had read an article in *The Swag Magazine*, by the Melbourne priest Eric Hodgens, which to some extent prepared me for what was coming. He wrote: 'The CDF is the current euphemism for the Inquisition. True to its mediaeval roots, it assumes the pope to be entitled to enforce his views. It conducts its delations [denunciations] and proceedings in secret. In today's secular world this is a violation of human rights. Theological censorship justifies itself as the quest for the truth and poses as truth's champion. In fact it is the enemy of the discovery of truth because discussion is forestalled. The contemporary secular world understands this and wisely enshrines freedom of speech and debate as a central value. The Church no less than any other enterprise is at least the poorer and at worst prone to error when it rejects this value. All of us are abused by this process.'

I was soon to realise the accuracy of what Hodgens had written. One evening my phone rang and my Redemptorist superior, the Irish provincial, Michael Kelleher, was on the other end of the line. He asked me to meet him the following day. At this stage I had spent more than a year as one of the leaders of the Association of Catholic Priests and we had experienced at first hand the difficulties priests had when allegations of child sexual abuse were made against them. Their stories had given me an insight into how a phone call from a bishop or religious superior could turn a priest's world on its head.

One of the things we quickly learned to do was to advise priests never to go to meet their bishop or superior without knowing the purpose of the meeting. The association had heard about some dreadful situations when a priest went to meet his bishop, expecting a chat about some aspect of his parish work, or maybe the possibility of being moved to another appointment, only to be confronted by the bishop, a canon lawyer and a child protection officer and told about an allegation of sexual abuse that had been made against him. In these circumstances the priest, in a state of shock, would be in no position to give due attention to his own rights under natural justice. And in some cases, after this traumatic meeting, he was left to drive home alone, sometimes considerable distances. It was a disgraceful way for the authorities to behave but at a certain stage it was a regular enough practice in some parts of the Irish Church. The only possible explanation for it was that the sense of panic that descended on the bishop or religious superior on receiving the allegation blinded them to the rights of the priest.

I was now in this situation: my superior was asking urgently to meet me. When I enquired of him what he wished to see me about he said he couldn't tell me over the phone. Even when I pressed him, he insisted that he could not tell me until we met. My caution about meeting him might seem strange to some readers but part of the reality of priests' lives today is that we are living with the constant threat of an allegation of some type of abuse or inappropriate behaviour being made against us, whether founded or unfounded. I asked my superior if an allegation of abuse had been made against me and, in fairness, he said that, if this were the case, he would not be asking to meet me on my own but advising me to bring someone with me to support me. But he continued to insist that he could not disclose on the telephone the purpose of the meeting he wished to have with me. At this point I became annoyed and ended the conversation by saying sharply that I would meet him only if I knew in advance the purpose of the meeting. I followed this up with an email to him stating this position. About twenty minutes later my immediate, local, superior rang to tell me the problem was that the Vatican had been in touch with our superior general in Rome objecting to some of my writings. On hearing this I felt a sense of fear and uncertainty.

The following day the superior general rang me from Rome. It was the first time in my life as a Redemptorist that I had got a phone call from, or indeed had any personal contact with, our top man in Rome. I knew straight away that this was serious. The superior, Michael Brehl, explained that he had received a letter from Cardinal Levada, the head of the Congregation for the Doctrine of the Faith, objecting to some of my writing. He said he could tell me no more, beyond the fact that I was in serious trouble and was required to go to Rome to meet him as soon as possible.

The Redemptorists currently have a total membership of more than five thousand priests and brothers throughout the world. We are made up of different units, known as provinces. Every six years delegates from all the provinces come together for a meeting, known as a chapter, which discusses relevant issues relating to the congregation and elects a superior general and a council who form the general government of the congregation for the following six years. Each province meets for a chapter every four years and elects a provincial and council to govern the province until the next chapter. It is a good system in that any individual serves in office only for a specified period of time, unlike bishops, who have indefinite tenure.

When I look back, it is clear to me that Michael Brehl felt under pressure from the CDF to get this matter sorted out and he passed the pressure on to me. There is a poem that says, 'Big fleas have little fleas//Upon their backs to bite 'em//And little fleas have lesser fleas,//and so, ad infinitum.' In my case the proverb could be inverted: I had the general of the Redemptorists on my back and he in turn had the CDF on his back. But I had no doubt where I stood; I was the lesser flea, at the end of the chain. The general stressed that the sooner I went the better, as he had international business on his schedule. I got a sick feeling in the pit of my stomach. This secrecy thing again! What was this awful accusation against me that could not be mentioned over the phone? Was it of such terrible moment that it would burn the telephone wires? Or was there a fear that the phone line to our remote monastery in the west of Ireland had been bugged? I had enough information to know for sure that my life was about to be turned upside down.

I know that many people experience this type of sudden and dramatic upheaval for different reasons, like losing their job or the death of someone close to them. It is not a pleasant experience. But it was compounded by the next part of the telephone conversation, which brought the secrecy factor to a whole new level. I was warned that I was not to tell anyone about the situation and this meant *anyone*, not even the people closest to me. I was now part of a process conducted by the Vatican according to their rules and the first rule I was ordered to observe was total secrecy. To violate this would be regarded as a very serious offence and would make my bad situation worse. As always with the Vatican, there was the implication that all their directives were enforced under pain of sin. I was catapulted into a world I had often read about and now I was going to learn about it close up and personal. To say the least it was disconcerting.

5

Summoned to Rome

The telephone conversation with the superior general and the summons to Rome constituted a major crisis for me. In order to cope, I broke the first rule of the institutional Church: I told people who were close to me. When I got the call I happened to be visiting one of my closest friends and I told her what I had just heard. Her immediate response was to say, 'Secrecy has always been the great weapon of the oppressor.' This comment freed me to discuss the situation with my family, my friends and some members of my Redemptorist community.

The Vatican argues that the purpose of such secrecy is to preserve the good name of the priest. The CDF sent a document to the Association of Catholic Priests in June 2012 that included this explanation: 'The CDF does not act "secretly" but through legitimate channels – in this case Father Flannery's superior general – in order to protect a priest's reputation where public notice may not be required.'

I do not accept that this is the real reason for the CDF's insistence on secrecy. If it were, surely it would be for the priest himself to decide if he wanted the matter kept secret or made public. As it happened, the CDF got extremely angry when my case was later made public. I believe that their concern is not likely to have anything to do with the good name of the priest but rather with their obsession with keeping their own archaic and unjust practices from being aired in public.

It is one thing to read about this type of thing happening to other people. But when it comes bursting into your own life it is very unsettling. Despite our awareness of the fragility and uncertainty of life, we inevitably plan out our future to a greater or lesser extent in our minds. We draw much of our security from our belief that we have our lives under control, from our knowledge of what we will be doing into the future. We hope that we will be able to continue in a meaningful occupation and weather any uncertainty that might come along the way. When something happens that puts all these plans in jeopardy one is left a bit like a boat on the ocean after the engines cut off. What is this going to do to my future? Will I be able to cope? Can my health survive the stress and pressure that are certain to accompany this?

On one level I have to acknowledge that this development should not have come as a great surprise to me. For more than twenty years I had been in the public eye, writing and speaking on various media outlets. I had written a number of books, some of which I knew were sailing close to the wind in relation to the hardline stances taken by the Vatican on certain issues in recent years. But I always felt that I was a small fish in a big pond and the fact that I was not an academic lecturing in some seminary or university meant that I would not be noticed – that I was not of any great significance where the Vatican was concerned. I remember a conversation I had about three years ago with the moral theologian, Sean Fagan, who has had great difficulty with the Vatican. He expressed surprise that I had not come to their notice. I said, 'Sean, you are an academic and I am only an ordinary preacher. They won't waste their time with me!'

I believe now that it was my involvement in the founding and leadership of the Association of Catholic Priests that changed the attitude of the Vatican towards me. While some commentators, especially the Catholic press in Ireland, might dismiss the association as the last kick of the generation of the 1960s, it developed rapidly, both in numbers and influence, and those of us in leadership consequently assumed a higher profile than before. As such I was more likely to draw attention to myself. The increasingly significant presence of a fairly aggressive conservative faction within the Irish Church, which had the ear of the Vatican and was more than willing to exploit it, was also something of which I was aware. In more recent years some of us Irish priests suspected that almost everything we said or wrote in public was relayed to the Vatican: for instance Owen O'Sullivan had already fallen foul of Rome for his writing on homosexuality. (Given what has recently been written about the growing number of gay men within the Catholic clergy and even the Vatican, this is loaded with irony.)

For the past twenty years or so we Redemptorists have tried our best to include lay people on our teams for mission work. Not only was our own manpower in decline, we were convinced that lay and clergy working closely together was the future of the Church. In the early days of this development we occasionally encountered a parish priest who did not want a lay person on the team but the large majority of people seemed to be very positive about it, although there were always some who believed that conducting church ceremonies was exclusively the work of the clergy. But in the past few years in particular some very militant lay people began to make life difficult for us. One morning at an early Mass on a parish mission, when the lay woman on the team stood up to read the Gospel before delivering the homily, two people came up the church, shouting, to stage a protest. We had no doubt that this was reported to the Vatican before the day was out.

The website of the ACP has been very successful. From the beginning we declared that everything we did would be reported on the site – that we would be completely transparent – and we have tried to keep to this. Someone in the know as regards the Vatican recently assured us that our website is carefully read on many computers in the Vatican each evening! But there was a couple of occasions when we breached our own rule of transparency. Trying to have any sort of meaningful meeting with the bishops has been enormously difficult, so when the Irish Bishops' Conference agreed to send two of their members to meet us we felt that this was worth pursuing, even though one of the conditions was that we would not publish a detailed account of the meeting but instead issue an agreed – and extremely bland – statement. Some of our members and contributors were not impressed – and rightly so!

The second occasion was a more recent meeting between the ACP and the Dublin Council of Priests, which included the highest-profile member of the Irish hierarchy, Archbishop Diarmuid Martin. It was decided that everything that was said at the meeting could be reported but that nothing would be attributed to any individual. It was frustrating that while Diarmuid Martin said some quite significant things at that meeting, they could not be attributed to him. A further difficulty with the transparency of our website is that sometimes we do not know who the contributors are, as they do not give their real names – a problem with all interactive websites. Given these limitations, the ACP website enables people of all shades of opinion to express their beliefs and views and it has become a serious vehicle for the discussion of religious issues.

As a result of my ACP experience of working with priests in trouble I knew I needed somebody with me when I went to Rome. My brother, two years older than me, with a lifetime of experience in business and politics, was happy to accompany me. A few days later, after I had made our travel arrangements, when I told the head of the Redemptorists in a phone call that I was bringing someone with me, I immediately sensed anxiety in his voice. He asked me if it was a legal person. (He was possibly aware that the ACP had the services of a legal team.) I explained that it was my brother and he told me that under these circumstances I could have permission to tell my brother about the situation.

Did he really believe that I had kept all this from my family for most of a week? Did he think that I had asked my brother to accompany me to Rome without explaining exactly why I was going? I was getting early insights into what can happen to a person when they assume a position of authority in the Church, especially when it comes to dealing with the Vatican. If I had kept these developments to myself rather than sharing them with people close to me, I would probably be going for psychological help rather than to a meeting in Rome. It was my first clear indication of the inhumanity of the processes engaged in by the Vatican and by those who carry out their orders. I was surprised and disappointed that the international head of the Redemptorists seemed to have bought into their way of thinking and acting.

I have been to Rome many times, both for meetings and on holiday, and it is a city I love, as so many others do, feeling that the title 'Eternal City' is not a misnomer. I have always been more at home in the historical quarters than in the Vatican. I love to stroll around the Colosseum and the Forum, or down by the Spanish Steps, thinking about the poetry of Keats and Shelley or watching life go by in the Piazza Navona. But heading out from Dublin on an early flight that Friday morning was a different experience. I felt burdened and fearful of what was ahead of me. For someone who grew up in the 1950s it is not easy to shed the fear of authority.

Our meeting with the superior general of the Redemptorists and his assistant was scheduled for two o'clock. When we landed at the airport there was one of those flash strikes which are such a feature of Rome, which meant that we were left sitting in the plane for over an hour before we managed to disembark. This did nothing to reduce my anxiety levels but we did eventually get to our destination in time for the meeting.

I had often been in the Redemptorist house in Rome but I had only briefly met the current superior general, Michael Brehl, on one of his visits to Ireland. He presented as a warm, pleasant, friendly Canadian and was in the third year of a six-year term as leader of the congregation. His background is more pastoral than academic and I suspected that he was not totally comfortable in the job. He met us at the entrance and brought us up to the part of the building where the general government offices are located. We were shown into a small conference room and put sitting around a table with Michael and his assistant, Enrique Lopez. Enrique, a native of Paraguay, is a small, jolly person.

After the usual chit-chat about travel and the frequency of sudden strikes in Rome and my introduction of my brother Frank, the meeting began. I was immediately told that I was in serious trouble and evidence of this could be deduced from the fact that three of the Vatican congregations had come together to deliberate about my case. I was also told that Cardinal Levada, head of the CDF, was personally to manage my case, which in the experience of Michael Brehl was very unusual. In this way, before I had time really to settle into my seat, I was told in no uncertain terms by both Michael and his assistant Enrique that my situation was very grave.

6

Two Documents

Michael handed across the table to me two A4 pages that had come from the CDF. The first one contained four extracts from articles I had written over the course of the previous two years in the Redemptorist magazine, *Reality*:

Quotes from Fr Tony Flannery CSsR, Published in *Reality*

April 2010: Fr Tony Flannery, CSsR, p. 20

Writing about structures of the institutional Church: 'Whatever Jesus intended, I don't think anyone can credibly claim that he intended the type of system we now have in the Church.'

July/August 2010: Fr Tony Flannery, CSsR, p. 20

'I no longer believe that the priesthood, as we currently have it in the Church, originated with Jesus. He did not designate a special group of his followers as priests. To say that at the Last Supper Jesus instituted the priesthood as we have it is stretching the reality of what happened. It is more likely that some time after Jesus, a select and privileged group within the community, who had abrogated power and authority to themselves, interpreted the occasion of the Last Supper in a manner that suited their own agenda.'

'I can no longer accept that interpreting the Word of God and celebrating the sacraments belong exclusively to the priesthood.'

Having quoted from Pope Benedict's 2010 letter to priests: 'Clearly, according to this quote, it is the priest alone who possesses the power to celebrate the Eucharist. There was probably a time when I believed that. But now I believe that the Word of God and the sacraments belong to and are already within the whole community, the Church, rather than the priest alone.'

November 2011, Fr Tony Flannery CSsR, p.14

'When I was young we looked to the teaching of the Vatican Council and were inspired by its vision. But the indications are that this is no longer the way the Church is going. The opposite appears to be the case. Instead of collegiality, the sharing out of decision making in the Church, we are becoming increasingly centralised. The power of bishops' conferences to make decisions has been curtailed more and more and everything is ultimately decided in the Vatican. After years of work promoting greater involvement in the liturgy, the new missal would seem to be a step back to the pre-Vatican II style of celebration, with the priest as the centre and the role of the people being downplayed.'

December 2011: Fr Tony Flannery, CSsR, p.14

'I suggested that as a result of the recent disclosures there were issues that the Church needed to take seriously, like compulsory celibacy as a condition for priesthood and the absence of a voice for women in decision-making at all levels of the Church but especially at the episcopal and Vatican level. I suggested that Catholic teaching of sexuality was in need of updating.'

On that day in the Redemptorist house in Rome I read down through these quotations and my initial reaction was that there was little enough there to justify my being considered to be in serious trouble – a good indication of how naïve I was in dealing with the Vatican. I had been a regular columnist with *Reality* magazine for twelve or thirteen years. As anyone knows who writes a regular column along with living a busy life, sometimes you put your column together at the last moment and maybe without the necessary editing, with the result that things are not always expressed as clearly and precisely as you might have wished. Furthermore, I am not a trained theologian and do not write with the sort of precision that theologians use. I have always been in the business of communicating with the ordinary Catholic, who has little or no theological training – partly because we in the Irish Church have never taken seriously the need for adult faith formation or theological education of the laity – so I try not to use words or sentences that would obscure meaning for them. Reading the four sentences that were now under the microscope I could see that in some cases I might have phrased things better and that my use of language in one or two instances was a bit loose. But this did not seem to justify my being ordered out to Rome at short notice and issued with such serious warnings.

My brother Frank, who had received some theological training in his early life, was even more nonplussed than me. Having read down through the page he said, 'This is the most pathetic rap sheet I have ever come across.' I wasn't familiar with the phrase and had to ask its meaning. (In case any readers are not familiar with this, it means a record of a person's crimes and convictions.) To his outsider's eyes, reading through this sheet, it seemed to be much ado about nothing.

Later, when I had the chance to check the full article of July-August 2010 from which the more problematic sentences were taken, I realised that when they were reinstated where they belonged, in the heart of the article, they had a very different meaning from that attributed to them when they were taken out of context.

I wrote this article after one of the state reports on clerical sexual abuse in Irish dioceses had been released, on this occasion the *Murphy Report* on the Dublin diocese. By this stage revelations of clerical sexual abuse had horrified the Irish people for a considerable period. Commentators at the time focused on what we call 'clericalism', the clerical culture and the 'group think' that prevailed within the Catholic clergy. Many experts saw this kind of group think as being responsible both for the abuse and – maybe even more so – for the cover-up. I had never been a fan of this type of clerical culture and my article was an expression of the damaging way in which I had experienced this culture and how I regarded it as a serious problem.

To say that Jesus did not intend the type of clerical system that had developed in the Church and caused so much damage was, I believed, fairly obvious. But I can also see that these sentences, isolated from their context, could take on a meaning that might be interpreted as heretical. I wonder if any of the staff of the CDF had read the full article, or taken any cognisance of the context in which it was written. In the aftermath of the *Murphy Report* Ireland was in a ferment of debate and discussion, of anger, vitriol and abuse of the clergy. It was an extremely difficult time for all priests. In order for someone properly to understand my article, it needed to be seen in this context. Of course I could have discussed all this in person with representatives of the CDF had I got the opportunity to meet them face to face but that is not how this body operates.

I felt from the beginning that if I had been able to sit down at the table, not with the messengers of the CDF – which is what the Redemptorist authorities effectively were – but with the people who were actually levelling these accusations against me and we had a reasonable discussion, we could have sorted the matter out very quickly. One possible solution was that I could have rewritten the offending articles more clearly and accurately for publication in *Reality*, with a note at the bottom stating that this rewriting was at the request of the CDF. But since then I have read Bradford E. Hinze (in *When the Magisterium Intervenes*, edited by Richard Gaillardetz) who gives a list of ten 'laments' by theologians about the way the CDF behaves in these situations. Number Seven is worth quoting:

'In those cases where a theologian is called to Rome for a colloquium with representatives of the CDF, there is a hope that some light can be shed on what many theologians believe are misunderstandings of their work – passages taken out of context, slanted interpretations and unfair implications attributed to the author. In fact what transpires is an interrogation in which the theologian is placed in the position of defending his or her position before a group of people who have already reached certain conclusions about what is required of the theologian, what positions must be repudiated, what innovations are deemed unacceptable. There is no possibility for mutual listening and learning to take place in this environment. There is no genuine dialogue.'

I was not even offered the opportunity of a colloquium with the CDF. I suppose that since I wasn't a professional theologian, they did not consider me worth it. But clearly the same background scenario prevailed. They had made up their minds about me and judgement had already been passed.

There was a further allegation, which was not written down but conveyed to me verbally by the Redemptorist superior general, that I had been quoted in a newspaper as having said that I would never use the word 'many' instead of 'all' in the words of consecration of the wine in the new translation of the missal. (*Take this all of you and drink from it, for this is the chalice of my blood...which will be poured out for you and for all [for many] for the forgiveness of sins.*') We in the Association of Catholic Priests had conducted a strenuous campaign against the introduction of the new missal, calling on the Irish bishops to postpone it until there was time to discuss it with the general membership of the Church. Our campaign got plenty of media coverage and I did some interviews on the subject. I quickly realised that, while there was no doubt that I had made this comment and that it represented where I stood on the matter, the research carried out by the CDF left a lot to be desired: they got both the newspaper and the date wrong, confusing two newspapers, *The Irish Times* and *The Sunday Times*. (I suspect that *The Irish Times* would be unhappy to be taken for a Murdoch newspaper!) Once I pointed out the inaccuracy this particular complaint was never mentioned again.

Then I turned to the second document, again an A4 page with no heading or signature:

The grave concerns of the Congregation for the Doctrine of the Faith concerning the publications and activities of Fr Tony Flannery, CSsR., a priest of the Irish province and a frequent contributor to both *Reality* and other publications. You are kindly requested to take the following steps (cf. *CIC* [*Codex Iuris Canonici/Code of Canon Law*] Canon 823, 1371.1 and 696.1):

The editor of *Reality* is to be instructed to immediately discontinue the regular monthly column written by Fr Flannery and published in that periodical.

You are to bring to the attention of Fr Flannery that the opinions expressed in his various articles published over the last two years in *Reality* are unacceptable. In particular, that the opinions expressed in his article entitled 'A Model in Need of Repair' (*Reality*, July/August 2010, p. 20) are clearly contrary to the defined teaching of the Church and call into question the nature of his own priestly ministry.

You are to seek to impress upon Fr Flannery the gravity of his situation and in order to assist him to re-embrace the full teaching of the Church; you are to impose upon him a period of spiritual and theological reflection at a location removed from his ordinary place of residence. During this period you are to encourage Fr Flannery to re-examine his religious vows and his duty as a religious priest to *sentire cum Ecclesia* [to 'think with the Church', in the words of St Ignatius of Loyola] (cf. *CIC*, Canon 601, 678.2,1319)

During this time, Fr Flannery is to be withdrawn from public ministry and is not to publish any further articles or give any interviews to the press.

You are to instruct Fr Flannery to withdraw from his leadership role in the Association of Catholic Priests.

I read down through this page with the sense that what I was looking at was a historical document from many centuries ago and simultaneously with the feeling that an enormous weight of authority of a type with which I was not familiar was coming down on top of me. I know that in the generations before my time as a priest the Redemptorists were a strict order and that the superiors had enormous power over the members. But this had all changed after the Second Vatican Council and I had lived through an era when the structures of governance in our congregation were very democratic. We had regular meetings at community and provincial level and all major decisions were made in consultation with the members. I had no experience of superiors throwing their weight around and laying down the law: if someone ever showed such tendencies he was not taken seriously. So the language of this document was a big shock: *'You are to seek to impress upon Fr Flannery the gravity of his situation.'* I had to pause and take a deep breath at this stage to remind myself that we were in the 21st century and not the 16th and that, despite the fact that the language and tone of this document came from that era, happily the Vatican no longer had the power to prepare the stake and fire for burning!

I read on. If anything, the language became even more dictatorial. The entire document was addressed not to me but to my Redemptorist superiors, which made for strange reading. I was the subject of this document, its content was to have an enormous impact on my life, yet I was being talked about in the third person. I was being reduced to an object, a passive recipient of other people's intentions and actions. The image of swatting a fly comes to mind: *'You are to instruct'*; *'You are to impose'*; *'In order to assist him to re-embrace the full teaching of the Church you are to impose upon him a period of spiritual and theological reflection at a location removed from his ordinary place of residence.'* While the opening paragraph included a request by the CDF to my order's superior general – *'You are kindly requested'* – the remainder of the unsigned document belied this. The superior general was not in reality being 'requested' to do anything; he was being told what to do.

The document made me very angry. I was in my mid-sixties and had spent almost fifty years in religious life, forty of them preaching the Gospel and working for the Church. I wondered who these faceless people were who had produced this document, on an A4 page with no heading or signature, containing these *diktats* that were to be imposed on me. Had any of them spent nearly forty years among the people, trying to make sense of the message of the Gospel in the modern world? Had they spent endless hours listening to the struggles of humanity? I suspected they hadn't. These documents were the work of people sitting in offices, divorced from ordinary life. Did I matter at all? They didn't seem to have the slightest interest in meeting me or hearing my side of the story. I was clearly of no consequence to them as a person. Was this the institution to which I had devoted my life? I read the final instructions. '*Fr Flannery is to be withdrawn from public ministry and is not to publish any articles or give any interviews to the press.*' I was to be silenced. And then the last straw: '*You are to instruct Fr Flannery to withdraw from his leadership role in the Association of Catholic Priests.*'

The passage of time gives us a better perspective on every event but I can still remember the feeling of oppression, even nausea, that settled over me on reading this document. I can clearly see the spotlessly clean but largely bare room, the pine table with nothing on it but the folders and notebooks people had brought with them to the meeting and the two sheets of white paper in front of me. I suspect that this image will be etched in my mind for ever. Of course I was in no fit state to have a detached and logical discussion on the content of the document or the implications of all this. I should have been given the documents well before the meeting, so that I would have had time to prepare myself. In this era of swift communication it would have been easy to email them to me and give me some days to reflect on them. But the ludicrous insistence on secrecy was used as the pretext for not doing something as simple as this.

The superior general and his assistant were pleasant, friendly men who gave us a great welcome. But I can see from the distance of more than a year that despite this friendliness they were part of a hard, rigid system that imposed rules and exercised old-style control. By accepting their positions they had signed up to the Vatican's way of doing things, which decreed that when it came to the test I as an individual would not be of any real significance.

Both the CDF and the Redemptorist general council would ultimately serve the system and if I threatened its authority I would be viewed as dispensable.

Even now, as I edit this book, reading through the page of *diktats* makes me angry again! I was lucky that I had my brother with me to support me at the meeting. Ultimately it is family that matters most in our lives.

7

The Origins of the Priesthood

Since the main issue that the CDF had objected to in my writings had to do with the origins of the priesthood, I will break temporarily from my narrative to give a brief sketch of some modern theological scholarship on this question. Let me say again that I am not a theologian, so this is by no means an exhaustive exposition of the subject.

'Priests' at the time of Jesus bore very little resemblance to modern Catholic priests as we know them. Their main work was servicing the temple in Jerusalem and organising all the temple activities, while Pharisees looked after the local communities and synagogues. Early Christians would not have been well disposed towards the Jewish priests, as it was they who, in the person of the High Priest Caiaphas, had Jesus arrested and brought before Pontius Pilate, demanding his death.

The New Testament reserves the word 'priest' for Jewish or pagan priests (only once is Christ called a priest, in the *Letter to the Hebrews*). The word is not used for Church officials. A notable development in the New Testament is that the Christian community, taking from the Old Testament the notion of the priest as the one who offers sacrifice, applies the word to itself, so that Christians are seen corporately as a group of priests who offer their bodies as a living sacrifice.

St Paul gives no clear indication about who presided at Eucharist in his time. But by early in the 2nd century Ignatius of Antioch gives witness to a clear organisation of one *episkopos* (overseer, bishop) and a group of presbyters and deacons in his city. This development became universal during the 2nd century but there was still no clear definition of roles, which were part of a fluid and evolving situation. From the 3rd century onwards the word 'priest' came frequently to be applied to bishops and later to presbyters. By this time it had become customary in the Church to have an ordination rite of presbyters by the laying on of hands. This style of ordination had now become normative and had won out over the more charismatic – less structured and less defined – model that had existed in Corinth. Clearly there was no single pattern of structure in the early Church; nor was there any common terminology to describe what did exist. The process of institutionalisation, the defining of roles and titles, was evidently a complex one that developed slowly and in different ways in different communities.

In the middle ages the idea of priesthood became intrinsically linked with that of ordained ministry. The developing concept of ordination focused attention on sacramental power (changing bread and wine into the body and blood of Christ, forgiveness of sin) and away from pastoral responsibility and relationship with a particular community or church. From this time on, the priest was no longer essentially part of the community. His main function became the celebration of Mass, with a lessening of emphasis on other community functions, and preaching was no longer central to his work.

The thinkers of the Reformation reacted against this development, insisting on the value of preaching and on the common priesthood of the faithful. In turn, the Counter-Reformation Council of Trent, in the 16th century, emphasised and defined the sacramental nature of priestly orders and taught that there is in the Church by the institution of Christ 'a new, visible and external priesthood, into which the old has been translated'. What they were attempting to do here was to emphasise that the priesthood had its origin in Christ and through Him in the ancient Jewish concept of priesthood.

In the 1960s the Second Vatican Council attempted to restore the concept of the link between the common priesthood of the baptised faithful and ordained ministry, although it noted that the ordained ministry is essentially different from that of the ordinary faithful. As in many other areas, the documents of the Council had a foot in both camps on this issue. It asserted that 'the divinely established ecclesiastical ministry is exercised on different levels by those who from antiquity have been called bishops, priests and deacons' but avoided a definitive pronouncement on the debate about whether the priesthood (not the episcopacy) was instituted by the apostles or, later, by the Church.

In the light of this complex historical process, how does the Church now understand the origin of priesthood? According to traditional Catholic theology the answer is clear and goes as follows: Jesus founded a new religion distinct from Judaism in his own lifetime. From among his followers he chose twelve apostles, gave them special training and named one of them, Peter, head of the Church. He also created the structural organisation of the Church, including offices and ministries with clearly defined authority. Some time before his death he instituted the sacraments of Eucharist and Holy Orders.

However, in the modern era of scholarship and with an educated laity, this traditional understanding is no longer historically credible. Using what in theology is called the 'historical-critical' method, we need to offer an account of the origins of priesthood – and of Church and papacy – that is both historically credible and faithful to Catholic convictions.

In an attempt at a more credible explanation, the theologian Richard McBrien writes of Jesus as *laying the foundations* for the Church rather than *founding* the Church. In a similar vein the distinguished scholar John P. Meier suggests an approach to the many historical developments out of which what we now call the papacy arose. He stresses that he believes this to have been an organic, generative process: not some historical accident or mistake but the expression of God's will and providence active in history – in other words, God reveals His plan for the world through the ordinary events of history and one of these pieces of history is the development of the papacy.

Addressing the question as to whether the papacy is of divine or human origin, another scholar, Walter Kasper, asserts that we do not require an explicit, historically obtainable saying by Jesus – in other words, his actual words – to describe what was intended. Instead we can understand and accept that the plan of God is being worked out in the historical and concrete developments of ministry in the Church. What has developed – based on the Scriptures, through the history of the Church and, it is hoped, under the guidance of the Holy Spirit – has become valid for the Church.

What McBrien, Meier and Kasper say about the Church and the papacy can be similarly applied to priesthood. Under the guidance of the Holy Spirit, in response to a changing historical situation (not least the growing numbers who became Christians) and following the command of Jesus to 'Do this in remembrance of me', the Church developed its ministry of priesthood, which historically has had many different forms.

A very important point emerges from all this, which explains what I was trying to touch on in the short article that I wrote for *Reality*: Jesus did not directly and explicitly institute priesthood in exactly the form that we know today and this gives us a certain freedom to adapt its form to present-day needs, trying always to be faithful to what is valid in Catholic tradition. For example, it seems that it was as late as the 5th century before distinctive garb indicated the difference between the clerical and lay state. We are conscious today that an exaggerated emphasis on the sacramental character of priesthood may have contributed to the clerical culture that I was writing about in my article, which has had many unwelcome effects.

In this context there is a renewed interest among those who are trying to re-establish the teachings of the Second Vatican Council in emphasising that baptism is the primary sacrament which establishes our equality as Christians and that it is better to view the sacramental character of Holy Orders as a leadership of service rather than with any sense of 'ontological' superiority ('ontological' means a fundamental change in the nature of the person who receives the sacrament).

In recent years scholars have been trying to explore more fully the intrinsic link between ordination and the common priesthood of the faithful, deriving from our baptism. This contemporary understanding of the historical development of the priesthood and its compatibility with basic Catholic teaching are the reasons I consider it wise and indeed necessary that the Church, in its teaching on priesthood and its origins, should acknowledge and incorporate the lengthy and often complex historical development that took place. To do otherwise is to ignore the needs of an educated 21st-century faithful.

Back to my narrative. After I had read the two documents in the Redemptorist headquarters in Rome, my superiors questioned me closely in relation to the quotations from my articles that the CDF had presented. The main focus was what I had said on the origins of the priesthood. Not having had any time to prepare myself, I could not refer to the article from which these sentences were taken or the context in which they were written. In matters like this, context is everything and fairness should have dictated that any such discussion would have taken place only if we had the complete article in front of us.

I could see that I had been touching on the theological debate that I have described, about the nature and origins of priesthood. Considering the difficulties the whole Church is experiencing around the notion of priesthood, from declining vocations to clerical sex abuse, it is only proper that this debate should be happening. Indeed it is inevitable. However, as I am not a theologian and my articles in *Reality* are written for ordinary churchgoing Catholics, I felt, perhaps wrongly, that it would not be appropriate or indeed possible to go into the details of this debate.

One of the big difficulties in the Church today is that much of what is written by scholars in the various branches of theology is not accepted by the Vatican authorities. They have assumed the right to decide what is permitted in theology and what is not and many commentators would say that for this reason Catholic theology over the past thirty years or so has lost most of the vitality and energy it possessed in the years after the Second Vatican Council. This is a great pity because it means that many of the good ideas introduced in the Council documents did not get the theological underpinning and development they needed and as a consequence have faded into insignificance.

Worse still, some of the scholars who have attempted something new and different have been censored in various ways but people like me read and study them because they come up with fresh and original ideas that make sense to us. Those of us who came to maturity after the Vatican Council have become used to theologians and scripture scholars pushing out the boundaries of knowledge and exploring new ways of looking at things and we find this stimulating.

The Church of our youth emerged from a period of three hundred years during which very little had changed. The Council of Trent, convened after the Reformation, was driven by the need to contradict and counteract the reformers, with the result that many things were set in stone and could not be revisited. The period from Trent until the middle of the twentieth century was in many ways one of stagnation in the Catholic Church. Apart from the most 'ivory towered' of academic circles, few new ideas permeated the body of the faithful, at least up until the early part of the twentieth century, and those few did not receive a warm welcome, as is evident in the Church's rejection of modernism and its *Syllabus of Errors.* For example, in the early twentieth century the Pope requested the Jesuits to expel one of their members, George Tyrrell, because of his views on modernism.

But when, in 1962, Pope John XXIII initiated the Second Vatican Council, saying it was time to 'throw open the windows of the Church and let the fresh air of the Spirit blow through', everything began to change. My generation was exhilarated and inspired by the new ideas and approaches. I suspect that many of us, including myself, would not have chosen priesthood but for the hope and promise of those days. When I was assigned to the monastery in Limerick for a period of two years prior to my ordination – a time when I was very unsure about my future – the community had a good number of young priests who were alive with new ideas and new ways of proclaiming the message. In a phrase that has often been used in recent times, the spirit of Vatican II was very evident there.

When John Charles McQuaid, then Archbishop of Dublin, came back from the Council in 1965 and announced to the Irish people that there would be no change to disturb them ('You may have been worried by much talk of changes to come. Allow me to reassure you. No change will worry the tranquillity of your Christian lives.') he had no idea of the type of revolution that would occur in the Redemptorists. I know we were by no means the only congregation to go through such a change but I was in the privileged position of being so engaged in it that it certainly influenced my decision to opt for ordination, something that directed the course of my life for the next forty years.

Looking back now I can see that there was a great deal of naïveté in us. We really believed that change had come to stay and that the ways of the past were no more. We failed to recognise that while the Council had produced a blueprint for a new way of being Church, it hadn't put the structures in place to make sure that the blueprint was implemented. We now recognise this as a crucial failure. All the documents in the world are of little use if the people in positions of power do not change their way of thinking and acting. I have lived to see a Church that is greatly different from what I thought it would be in those heady days of my youth. Recently a young Redemptorist, admittedly not of the Irish province, celebrated a major jubilee Mass in Latin with his back to the people. The old adage, 'You cannot turn back the clock' may be in the process of being disproved within the Catholic Church!

Since the inauguration of John Paul II in 1978 and the beginning of what is now generally referred to as the 'reform of the reform', a big effort was made to put a halter on the academics who were writing books on Scripture and theology and filling our heads with new ways of looking at things. Gradually theology settled back into a more traditional mode, sticking closely to the official positions of the Church on all issues. Scripture scholars began to be more curtailed in what they wrote. When that happened many people of my generation began to look elsewhere for understanding and inspiration. We turned more to those who were writing from the fringes, people like Charles Curran and Hans Kung, who had been banished from Catholic seminaries and universities, later to the liberation theologians and more recently to people like José Pagola, as well as writers from the other Christian Churches.

Really interesting material about the origins of the Church and the early years of its development was appearing. By means of new interpretations of the New Testament, we learned to distinguish between what may have been the authentic words of Jesus and the words of the early Church communities where the gospels originated. We learned that these early Christian communities had specific human agendas that influenced how they told the stories, although this does not in any way suggest that the Scriptures are not the inspired word of God. These developments meant that we interpreted the Scriptures in a much less literal sense than previously.

There were many priests who read and studied these writers but believed that they should not refer to them in their preaching. They continued to observe the principle that the simple faith of the people should not be disturbed. But I have always believed that I should introduce some of these ideas in my preaching, that what was being discussed in theological circles should be made accessible to the people in the pew. I recently heard a searching, educated and practising Catholic describe his faith formation as being 'educated into simplicity'. This kind of formation is no longer adequate. In our society most people have a high standard of education and it would be wrong to treat them like children and not allow them the opportunity to look at the Catholic faith and Catholic tradition in new ways.

Nor is there always a dichotomy between faith and reason: in fact I have always believed that faith needs to be bolstered by reason. This is why I wrote about issues like the origins of Church and priesthood. I believed it would be wrong to leave people with the impression that Jesus ordained his disciples at the Last Supper in the same way that priests are being ordained today. They needed to know that the matter is much more complex than that. There was also a need to teach that Jesus preached about the Kingdom of God rather than the Church and that many scripture scholars suggest that the two mentions of 'Church' in the Gospel are in all probability later additions.

One of the consequences of this way of thinking was to raise questions about what, if anything, was the kind of Church intended by Jesus, or if it was his intention to found a Church at all. It was my discussion of these very issues in my articles in *Reality* that the CDF objected to. Recently the Vatican has made great efforts to suppress these sorts of ideas and to confine its thinkers and writers rigidly to the official line. Bradford E. Hinze expresses it well:

'Theologians who are working in the Church at the frontiers of theology are being held to doctrinal definitions and standards that are treated as frozen in time by means of ahistorical positions. In areas where dramatic doctrinal developments are occurring, the CDF is judging people using a strict and often narrow propositional approach to doctrinal formulations. Dogmatic propositions are treated as rigid rules, rather than as living tradition. There is too little acknowledgement of the fact of doctrinal development and of the hierarchy of truths. There is no acknowledgement of the fact that certain doctrines are widely contested among bishops, clergy, lay faithful and theologians. Often there is an attempt to elevate non-infallible teachings to infallible norms by papal or curial edicts. From this concern results the widespread charge of creeping infallibilism.'

This is exactly the type of trouble I ran into. What I perceived as a topic widely debated in Church circles became, as soon as the CDF began to deal with it, 'frozen in time'. It is impossible for my generation of Catholics, who have lived our lives comfortable with and excited by new insights, to go back to the old ways of rigid orthodoxy. I now found myself personally involved in the anomalous situation that exists in the Church, sitting, without preparation, in front of the two highest-ranking officials of the Redemptorists, while these few sentences I had written on the origin of priesthood were scrutinised.

Recently the American historian Garry Wills published a book on priesthood, entitled *Why Priests? A Failed Tradition*. It is interesting in the context of my situation to note some of the things he says in this book. In her very positive review of the book in *The Irish Times*, theologian Linda Hogan makes the following comments:

'There is scarcely a mention of priesthood in the New Testament. Nor is the phenomenon of priesthood evident in the practices of the early Church. How then, asks Garry Wills, did the priesthood become so central to Christianity, and particularly to the Roman Catholic Church, and why is there such an attachment to its continuation in a religion that began without it?'

'Wills describes the early Christian community as "a priestless movement" that was essentially egalitarian.

'The writer of the *Letter to the Hebrews* describes Jesus as a priest in the line of Melchizedek (a Caananite king referred to in the *Book of Genesis*) and over the centuries, from this idiosyncratic text, the Church began to construct an account of priestly power which implied that the priesthood was established by Jesus and that his apostles could also be understood in priestly terms. This, Wills insists, is quite simply false. It has no historical basis.

'According to Wills, in the early Church, "there were no priests and no priestly services; there was no re-enactment of Jesus's Last Supper; no 'sacrifice of the Mass'; no consecration of bread and wine; nothing that resembled what priests now claim to do." There is no doubt that, when taken together, such claims appear to be radical. However, much of the historical and theological analysis on which Wills builds his thesis is uncontroversial among scholars.'

It is clear from this brief review of Wills's book that the few relatively harmless comments of mine to which the Vatican objected pale into insignificance compared to what is being written by some modern scholars. (Of course, Wills, being a layman, is more independent of Church authority!) I am not suggesting that everything Wills says is accurate, or that I agree with it. But he is a serious scholar of Church history who cannot easily be dismissed.

Such scholarship shows clearly that the era in which the Vatican could control the dissemination of ideas is well and truly over. To quote an Irish politician of some years ago: 'They are trying to keep out the tide with a fork.'

8

A 'Political' Strategy

Despite the fact that I was not in the ideal frame of mind to have such a serious discussion, there was clearly no question in the minds of my Redemptorist superiors but that the discussion would continue. After questioning me closely on my views, Fathers Brehl and Lopez eventually concluded that I wasn't really a heretic. I found it hard to take this part of the discussion seriously because, while I might have thought of myself as being slightly left of centre I never considered myself particularly extreme. But these two men, who work in Rome and are familiar with Vatican politics, said that convincing the CDF would be a much more difficult matter, that different, obscure standards applied there. They warned me again that I was in serious trouble with the people who had the real power in the Church.

There was a short break in our meeting, when Frank and I were left alone to absorb what we had heard over a cup of coffee. I was still in a state of shock, more as a result of the language of the two documents that had been presented to me than their content. My memory of our chat at this time was that while I was angry and in the mood for confrontation, Frank was already beginning to work on how the situation might be handled. In a little while the two Redemptorists returned and the discussion resumed. With his background in business and political strategy, Frank now took the lead in the discussion and immediately began to outline possible ways of moving forward. He has a logical mind and plenty of experience of sorting out difficult situations.

Michael Brehl was happy with the direction the discussion had taken. Together he and Frank set about working out a process whereby the Vatican could be persuaded to deal leniently with me. They agreed that if they could devise a strategy, a process, and propose a series of steps to be taken, the problem would become more manageable and it would be possible to solve it. This was not really what I wanted to hear. I was angry and disorientated by what I had read and felt like telling my superiors to go back to the CDF with the message that this whole episode was a charade and that I did not want to play their power games. But I had enough sense to keep silent for the most part and let the discussion go on around me.

I recognised that Michael Brehl and Frank had developed a certain rapport. They were able to speak the same language, the language of political strategy. Despite my anxious state, I saw with some amusement how these two people, one from the secular world and the other from the religious, so rapidly found a common ground, relying on a common set of skills. It dawned on me that dealing with a political party or a government and dealing with the Vatican bureaucracy weren't really that different, except of course that citizens have a voice in electing a government. Looking at it now from the distance of more than a year and taking into account all that has happened in the meantime, I realise that dealing with the Vatican was in fact a different reality. The CDF operates on the basis of concepts and procedures that were dispensed with in civil and political society centuries ago.

While all this was going on, I, with little experience of political manoeuvring and with what I can now see were fairly naïve views on freedom of speech and the dignity of the human person, was a bit lost. My memory of the meeting, which lasted for about three hours, is that it seemed to go on outside me, as if I were just an observer. We did produce a strategy, a process. I was willing to go with the *diktats*, to take the period of time for 'theological and spiritual reflection' but I was uneasy about leaving Ireland as had been recommended. The notion of being driven out of my own country by Vatican officials was a bridge too far for me. To be fair to Michael Brehl he did not put too much pressure on me about this. I would refrain from writing or any media involvement during this time but I would not resign from my leadership role in the ACP. I felt that this was a crucial issue and that I had to take a stand on it because, if I conceded and stood down on orders from the Vatican, we as an association would be conceding our status as an independent body. If we did this we would very rapidly become subservient and the other leaders could also be targeted. Brehl said that he would attempt to renegotiate this condition for me. I said that while I was willing to take the time out, I knew very clearly that I would not be able to *sentire cum Ecclesia*, as they wished, because I firmly believed that current CDF thinking was not for the good of the Church. I did find my voice to say that I did not think that a hundred years of 'spiritual and theological reflection' would get me into the space of accepting it.

It was agreed that I would work as normal until Easter, which was about six weeks away, as I was already committed to work on parish missions and going off to reflect at this time would cause problems for the mission team (our greatly reduced resources mean that getting substitutes at the last minute would be very difficult). After Easter I would be out of ministry and away from my normal residence until the end of May. A spiritual director would be appointed to accompany me during this period. At the end it was hoped that I would be in a position to write a statement for publication that would satisfy the CDF that I was not a heretic or that if I had been on my way to becoming one I had repented and returned to the fold! The meeting ended with Michael Brehl assuring me that he would shortly be meeting Cardinal Levada and that he would do his best to argue my case and reassure the Vatican.

One thing that was obvious from beginning to end of the meeting was that the real power in this matter was not in the room. At no stage was there even a hint of the Redemptorist authorities standing up to the Vatican on any significant issue or refusing to implement what had been ordered. Certainly they were more than willing to speak on my behalf and do their best to mitigate the sentence but this was as far as they could go. In the end the Vatican had all the power and there was an unspoken assumption that we had to bow our heads and accept.

To my surprise I also realised that while I, of the three 'Church' people around the table, was the only one not in a position of authority, I was the one with the greatest freedom of action. I could submit to what they were asking of me or I could walk away and refuse. The other two men, precisely because of their positions of power, however limited and curtailed this power was, had little choice but to go along with the orders they got from the other side of the Tiber. The general assumption was that, if they refused, the CDF could easily ask for their resignation and they would have to comply, although, as the process went on, I did wonder about the accuracy of this assessment. Whereas I had really only myself to think of, their actions could have serious consequences for the whole Redemptorist congregation. Power is a strange thing: sometimes the people who seem to have most actually have least.

During the meeting both Frank and I emphasised that if this matter came to the notice of the media in Ireland it would get a lot of publicity and have the potential to generate much negative reaction to the institutional Church. It would further damage the image of the Vatican, already very low in Ireland for several reasons, notably the handling of the clerical sex abuse issue. We stressed that if I were to stand down from leadership of the ACP it would inevitably bring the issue into the public domain and warned that as a member of that association I was in the unusual position (for a priest) of having a high-powered legal team on which I could call to contest the case. My intuition was that this was not taken too seriously but I believe that later events proved me right. I don't think they considered that what they were involved in had any relation to civil authority. The meeting ended with my superior emphasising yet again the crucial importance of keeping the whole matter under a veil of strict secrecy.

There was an interesting sub-text to all this. On 20 July 2011, the Irish Taoiseach, (prime minister) Enda Kenny, delivered a speech in the Dáil (parliament) that was highly critical of the Vatican for failing to deal adequately with the clerical sexual abuse scandal in Ireland or cooperate with the Irish state in the matter. It was an extremely strong speech and many commentators opined that it was a watershed in Irish Catholicism, being the first time since the foundation of the State in 1922 that an Irish leader had spoken out against the government of the Church. It was even more surprising as Kenny himself is a practising Catholic and would not be viewed as one of the burgeoning number of anti-Church politicians. While some suggested that the speech was opportunistic, given that Church support was by then at an all-time low, it was very well received by the majority of the people. It came at a time when yet another report, this time from the diocese of Cloyne, had shown up serious failures in the way the Church had handled clerical sexual abuse in the diocese.

The Irish Times asked me to write a response to Enda Kenny's speech, which was published the following day. I was largely supportive of what the Taoiseach had said, believing he had accurately expressed the feelings of most Irish people at that time. The Vatican reacted angrily to the speech and some Catholic spokespeople in Ireland were outraged. Gradually I began to hear it rumoured that I had written the speech for Enda Kenny. Apparently the fact that I had given a positive response to the speech and the fact that my brother had worked for the Taoiseach's political party, led people to put two and two together and get at least five. There was no substance at all to the rumour but it was wheeled out by some media people as the reason for my becoming a target of Vatican disapproval. Sometimes even the media get things wrong!

9

A Deep and Opaque Mist

We returned to Ireland the following morning and I went straight into a parish mission in north Mayo, feeling quite disoriented. Missions are a type of evangelical event and they are largely what I have spent my life working on. A team of us, Redemptorist and lay, go to a parish, usually at the invitation of the pastoral council. We spend a period of time there, maybe one or two weeks, during which time we invite people to come to church each day, morning and evening, and we present the message of the Gospel using various techniques of communication, from traditional preaching to music and drama. The purpose of missions is to renew and reinvigorate the faith of a parish community.

On this occasion I was staying with the parish priest, a good, decent man, in a house that looked out on the Atlantic. I can remember during those first days pacing up and down my bedroom and standing at the window looking out. The days were wet and dark and the sky was almost on the ground, as it can be in the west of Ireland, so I could barely make out the sea, even though it was only about a hundred yards away. I was looking into a deep and opaque mist and it was a real case of pathetic fallacy, the weather reflecting my emotional state. I was trying to get my mind around the situation. I believe that I am normally a reasonably calm and placid individual (others may not agree) but during those days my emotions were in turmoil and I think I had periods of depression that affected my sleep, my appetite and my energy levels.

During this period not only had I to go out and preach, I was responsible for leading the mission team. My colleagues were a recently ordained Redemptorist priest and a young lay woman.

With the decline in faith and the demoralised state of the Church, religious practice in Ireland has fallen sharply. For a mission to be a success it is necessary to come in with great energy and enthusiasm, so that the message can go out that this is not just more of the same but something new and fresh. I wasn't exactly in the right frame of mind on this occasion. When I was carrying out my mission duties, preaching or saying Mass, it took an enormous mental effort to block out what had happened in the previous few days and get on with the work. The message I had been preaching at these events for many years, a message of God's love and compassion for his people, a message of freedom, stood out in stark relief against this new background and I began to question if I believed it any more.

My colleagues on the team quickly recognised that something was amiss and one of them asked me if anything was wrong. The question freed me to speak – it was almost as if it were giving me permission to break the secrecy order, to which I had little or no commitment. I explained the situation both to my colleagues on the team and to the parish priest. I also acquainted my co-leaders in the ACP of the situation and showed them the two documents.

Despite all the tension I felt, despite the weather, the mission in north Mayo was good for me. It forced me out of myself and helped me to get over that first crucial week. During the next number of weeks I was involved in various kinds of work and gradually got myself back on to an even keel. I came to the conclusion that, no matter what the outcome, I would be all right. I found some solace in the famous line from Julian of Norwich: 'All shall be well and all shall be well and all manner of things shall be well.' I began to regain control of the situation. My anger with the Vatican persisted but I reminded myself that I was willing to go along with the process as agreed.

Throughout Lent I continued to work on missions with other Redemptorists and I made no effort to keep the situation secret from them. I suspect it would not have been possible anyway, since they would easily have guessed there was something the matter. Someone once said that once two people know something, that something is no longer a secret! Inevitably, Ireland being a small country, my 'something' was going to get to the media eventually and when *Reality* came out without my usual column it was even more likely to happen. Coming towards Easter there were indications that some media people had got a smell of the story and it eventually broke on Holy Thursday. (The fact that the *Irish Catholic* was the first to get the story and that it regularly boasts of having a 'senior source' in the Vatican raises the possibility that the leak might have come from there, a minor addendum to the Vatileaks scandal!) I refused all interviews, saying that I had given a commitment that I would not speak publicly on the matter at this time. Still the story took off and I can recall feeling that it was almost surreal when I heard it being announced to the nation on the nine o'clock evening news on television.

The news received some international attention and here in Ireland it was given oxygen by the leaking of information about various other priests who had been censored in different ways. The fact that I was no longer writing for *Reality* also led to the breaking of the story that *Reality* was censored and could no longer carry articles about certain topics: the ordination of women, compulsory celibacy, homosexuality, criticism of the Pope and, somewhat surprisingly, general absolution. It emerged that Brian D'Arcy, a Passionist priest and well-known columnist and commentator on religious affairs, had had a censor appointed to monitor his writing and media work. Brian has been writing for a Sunday tabloid newspaper for many years. His columns are usually light and snappy, as suits the publication. He has great skill at this, managing to communicate effectively with people who are not normally touched by the Church. Most people considered that the censoring of Brian D'Arcy was both stupid and unnecessary. Commentators recalled that the Capuchin priest, Owen O'Sullivan, had been censored for an article he wrote in *The Furrow* on the Church's teaching on homosexuality.

But the saddest story of all had to do with the moral theologian, Sean Fagan, who is a Marist priest. Sean is in his mid-eighties and in bad health. He had been silenced some years earlier because of his book, *Does Morality Change?* The Vatican ordered the Irish bishops to have the book withdrawn from circulation. Incredibly (or maybe not) his religious superiors went to the shops and to the publishers and bought up all remaining copies of the book, reputedly more than eight hundred. Sean does not know what happened to them but at the time of writing he tells me that one second-hand copy of the book is on sale on the internet for a few hundred euro! Sean was also ordered not to write or speak publicly and threatened that if he revealed the sentence that had been imposed on him, he would be dismissed from the priesthood. For Sean, even at this stage of his life and with failing health, the priesthood was important, so he largely, although not completely, observed the restrictions. He had given his story to a journalist, with instructions that it be published only after his death. But when my situation became public he gave the journalist permission to publish his story.

I can recall my reaction when I first heard Sean's story on a visit to his room in the Marist residence about three years ago. He showed me all the medicine he was taking, something like twenty-two tablets every day, and even so he was in a great deal of pain. He seemed weak and old. I asked myself, 'How could the powers in the Vatican possibly do something like this and believe they are acting in the name of Christ?' It was a shocking story and when it emerged it caused great dismay around Ireland.

When the various tales of censorship surfaced there was enough oxygen to keep the story going for about two weeks. It was a strange experience for me to find myself discussed in the media while remaining silent, as I had agreed. But this turned out to be of great benefit as it gave me an opportunity to reflect on what had happened, to consider my own beliefs and values and to figure out the important issues in life generally and in my life in particular. Engaging in public debate during those weeks would have prevented me from distilling what I had experienced to the essential question I was facing: what price would I be willing to pay in order to continue as a practising priest, preaching missions and novenas.

The two weeks or so that these stories ran prominently in the media were a negative time for the public image of the Vatican in Ireland. Its image was already poor due to the accumulation of events over the previous twenty years but when the treatment of priests who asked questions became known, it was a further serious blow. The Vatican came across as a bully, an institution that had really not changed very much since the 16th century. Virginia Satir, one of the pioneers of family therapy, wrote in her book, *Conjoint Family Therapy*, that dysfunctional people have difficulty with difference. The Vatican certainly has a problem with difference.

Most people nowadays take freedom of speech for granted and even the most traditional of Catholics were amazed that this repression of divergent views could happen in today's world. There were, of course, others who were quite pleased and said publicly that it was past time this had happened. Some people, who themselves were involved in the public domain, in politics and journalism, and who would have been appalled if someone had tried to limit their freedom to speak, expressed approval of what the Vatican was doing. They did it on the basis that in the Church there is only one authority, the Pope, and if everyone were allowed to have their own opinion and express it, we would turn out like Protestants and 'look what has happened to them'. Some even suggested that I should go off and become a Protestant, as if this were a fate worse than death. I considered this to be quite offensive to our Protestant sisters and brothers.

On the other hand, I began to receive a great volume of letters, emails, texts and phone calls from people offering their support and wishing me well. I was quite surprised by this. I had no idea that my speaking and my writing had helped so many. Mostly these messages expressed the view that the institutional Church was out of touch with people's daily lives. Some older people expressed regret that the Church was failing to speak to the next generation. These messages of support were very important in helping me to cope and encouraging me to keep faith in myself, in my beliefs and in who I am as a person. One particularly poignant note read: 'You will have to wait to see who you are when this thing is done with you.' This reminded me that I was in a life-changing situation, that this experience would have a profound effect on me.

I got great support from my own colleagues in the Redemptorists. One incident that stands out for me is a phone call I received from one priest in his late eighties. He strongly encouraged me to stick to my guns and not to give in to what he regarded as oppressive and unjust treatment. A few of my colleagues were particularly angry with the Vatican and in various ways made their views public, through interviews or letters to the paper.

But Big Brother had not gone away, something that was to have repercussions before too long. Another aspect of these weeks of media exposure was also to have repercussions. The fact that I was not giving interviews meant that I could have no influence over what was being published. The media, by its nature, tend to go for the more sensational angles and some articles gave the impression that the Vatican was silencing me because of my views on women priests and moral questions, even though these issues did not feature in the original complaints. The following September the Vatican used this as a pretext to add them to the list of issues about which it required me to publish a statement of retraction.

10

Spiritual and Theological Reflection

I began my period of 'spiritual and theological reflection' after Easter, as I had been ordered to do by the CDF. Even though Fr Brehl had urged me to spend this period outside Ireland I did not leave the country. He had suggested that I should go to a retreat centre, maybe in England or the west coast of America. Under normal circumstances, a couple of months on the west coast of the US would have been very desirable but I felt that if I went abroad at this point it would seem that I had been banished from Ireland by Rome, so I was not willing to go. I needed the advice and support of my family and friends if I were to write a statement for the CDF. I had more faith in their guidance than I would have in the counsel of a canon lawyer or theologian whom I had never met before and who would more than likely be immersed in Church politics.

I also had the sense that the idea of packing up and leaving Ireland at very short notice is very far removed from the reality of the lives of ordinary people. Not too many people in the pews can decide on the spur of the moment to spend six weeks in California. To some extent the very suggestion that I should do so is a sign of the disconnect between Church leaders and the average churchgoer.

Instead I went to live in my old family home, where I had spent such a satisfying sabbatical year after I had completed my term as superior of one of our monasteries and where I had written my first book. This time it did not disappoint. April and May are probably the nicest months of the year in Ireland and it was lovely to have the time to myself without the pressure of preaching missions and novenas.

I kept to my agreement not to publish or speak to the media but

I did not pull back from my work with the ACP. Since our inception in 2010 we had been calling for some form of assembly that would give a forum to ordinary lay Catholics to express their views about the crisis being experienced by the Irish Church. We were aware that there had been rumblings that the Irish hierarchy were considering such a move but, for whatever reason, they did not initiate any step in this direction. I expect they were nervous of what would come out of such a gathering and that it would get them in trouble with the Vatican, since some of the topics that were 'off the agenda' would inevitably appear.

In the absence of any other initiative we decided to go ahead and organise something ourselves. A proper representative assembly of the Irish Church would have needed a degree of planning and preparation that was beyond our capacity, so we decided to call our gathering 'Towards an Assembly of the Irish Church'. The date we arranged for the event was in early May 2012, which was right in the middle of my period of 'reflection'. The initial *diktat* from the CDF – that I step down from my leadership role in the ACP – had been temporarily suspended, although I was supposed to refrain from involvement during this period of reflection. But from the beginning I was involved in the nitty-gritty of planning the event and there was no way I was going to back out of it. We all recognised its importance and felt that it was crucial that it be a success if an alternative voice were to be raised in the Irish Church.

We held the assembly at a hotel in Dublin. We expected a couple of hundred people to attend but we had to close down the registration facility a week before the event was due to take place because we had reached the maximum number for which the hotel could cater. In the end close on twelve hundred people came and the day was an enormous success. There was a tremendous sense of energy and enthusiasm and people who attended felt encouraged and supported in their beliefs about their Church and their faith. Most were of the older generation, those who grew up with Vatican

II. What was really significant was that they were still excited by the vision of those years and had kept their enthusiasm for the struggle to bring this vision to reality. To look around an assembly of people, mostly with greying or balding heads, and witness their excitement as they listened and spoke was really remarkable. The very fact that so many other people shared a sense of unhappiness about the way the Church was being governed was a great boost to us all. There was a small number of younger people present and, by and large, they were of a different mindset. For them adherence to official Church teaching seemed to be the only thing that mattered.

The assembly got extensive media coverage and while I did not give any interviews I was photographed and appeared in some of the newspapers the following day. It was a strange day for me, as so many people took the trouble to meet me and wish me well. Their message was clear: 'Don't back down; stick to your guns'! Instinctively I knew that any statement I prepared for the CDF could not be a fudge. From a public relations point of view it was a good day for the ACP and not so good for the CDF. The bishops did not come well out of it either. Though they had been invited none of them turned up and neither, of course, did the new Papal Nuncio.

Their attitude was hard to understand. The event was within walking distance of both the Nunciature and the residence of the Archbishop of Dublin. It was not a heretical or divisive group but a large gathering of committed Catholics, almost all of them likely to be regular in their attendance at Sunday Mass. It would have been hard to imagine a less threatening gathering. There was no danger that anyone was going to throw rotten eggs at the bishops. These people had gathered because they loved the Church and were disturbed by what was happening to it. If a bishop had shown up even for a short while and come to the microphone and wished us well on the day, the gesture would have been very well received.

The absence of the bishops raises questions. Are they afraid? If so, what are they afraid of? The tide is going out for the Church in this country and now more than ever is a time for courage and unity to face the difficult times ahead. One senior member of the hierarchy who replied to our invitation wrote about the importance of what he called *'communio'*, the idea that Catholics should be in communion, united with one another. He seemed to be implying that by calling this gathering we were showing ourselves not to be in communion. For him *communio* seemed to mean following a certain line and leaving no room for people to question official Church positions on any issue.

Whatever the reason, the bishops all chose to stay away. I presume they felt that they might have to face questions to which the Vatican did not permit them to give any answer except the official one. It is probable that some of them, in their hearts, do not really believe these official answers either, so they may have stayed away to avoid embarrassment. It was a missed opportunity.

At this stage the Association of Catholic Priests had been in existence for almost two years. We had already clearly demonstrated that we were very different from the National Conference of Priests, which had finally been disbanded in 2007 due to lack of interest. One well-known anecdote from that period concerns an occasion when the head of the NCPI went to meet the then Papal Nuncio, Giuseppi Alibrandi. The Nuncio told him, in words that surely deserve to go down in history, that he was 'a nobody, representing nobodies'. After that spectacular day in Dublin it was clear that the ACP was 'somebody', representing a great number of the Catholic faithful, both lay and clergy. The day could not have been such a success if we were not an independent body, a reality which is most unusual among priests' organisations.

Down through history the Church has always tried to keep a tight rein on its priests. One of the most significant ways of doing this, of course, was the imposition of compulsory celibacy, as it is much easier to control a single man than one with a wife and children. The priests were always seen as the servants of the institution, the men on the ground who kept the system running smoothly and implemented the orders that were handed down from on high. Without an obedient and docile priesthood it would be hard for the Church to function as it does today, so an independent body of priests was clearly something that was not within the comfort zone of the Church authorities.

It has become very obvious over the past few years that the Irish bishops are unsure how to deal with this new, independent body. At one of our meetings Michael Brehl quoted Cardinal Levada as stating that he did not have a problem with the ACP but I find it hard to believe that I would have been targeted by the CDF had I not been in a leadership position in that organisation. It could be pointed out that the three other leaders of the ACP did not fall foul of the CDF and it may be that the CDF tactic was to 'take out' one of us, so as to 'put manners on', or even frighten the others.

Until recently the Irish bishops have consistently refused to come to ACP meetings or have any sort of meaningful dialogue with us. As I write this account we are engaging in a series of meetings with diocesan priests' councils, with the local bishop present. The Bishops' Conference offered us this forum when they refused to meet us as a body. We did have a meeting with two bishops, representing the Conference, in early 2012 but while it was pleasant and sociable it was a private meeting and afterwards the only statement we were allowed to release was one that contained the usual platitudes, giving no hard information.

This meeting took place during the early stages of my difficulties with the CDF and if I am honest I have to admit that I went along with this half-hearted effort at dialogue because it was good optics in Rome. The Redemptorist superiors were more than pleased with the idea that the ACP was meeting Irish bishops and I was told that this would be very significant in negotiations with Cardinal Levada. But there was no real exchange of ideas. The interesting thing was that, in the privacy of the hotel room where we sat around a table, it was evident that there was little enough difference of opinion between ourselves and the two bishops. But they were totally constrained by their role.

I left that meeting with the distinct impression that the ACP was in a far greater position of influence than the Catholic hierarchy because we were able to speak our minds publicly. This need not be the case. If the Irish bishops were willing to come together as a bishops' conference and make some joint decisions they could become very powerful. If, for instance, they had agreed that they would not use the new missal, there is very little the Vatican could have done about it. It couldn't sack them all. As there was so much dissatisfaction with the new missal among priests, it was the perfect opportunity for the Irish Church to take a stand. There was nothing doctrinal at stake and consensus would have been easy to achieve. All that was missing was the support of the bishops.

But there is no possibility of the bishops taking a stand. The Irish Bishops' Conference is a dysfunctional body and there is no real leadership. The one among the bishops who has most capacity to lead is Diarmuid Martin, Archbishop of Dublin, but for whatever reason he has not assumed this role.

We are paying the price for a long period during which episcopal appointments were made for all the wrong reasons. Men were chosen not for their leadership ability but for their orthodoxy. If the main criterion for choosing bishops is their full acceptance of the Vatican point of view on married priests, homosexuality and contraception, it is very unlikely that we will get independent people, with the ability and strength of character to give real leadership.

11

The ACP Enters the Fray

When the news about my difficulties with the CDF broke in April the leadership of the ACP issued a statement.

'The Association of Catholic Priests (ACP) is disturbed that Fr Tony Flannery, a founding member of the Association, is being "silenced". We believe that such an approach, in its individual focus on Fr Flannery and inevitably by implication on the members of the association, is an extremely ill-advised intervention in the present pastoral context in Ireland.

'We affirm in the strongest possible terms our confidence in and solidarity with Fr Flannery and we wish to make clear our profound view that this intervention is unfair, unwarranted and unwise. The issues surfaced by the ACP since its foundation less than two years ago and by Tony Flannery as part of the leadership team are not an attack on or a rejection of the fundamental teachings of the Church. Rather they are an important reflection by an association of over 800 Irish priests – who have given long service to the Catholic Church in Ireland – on issues surfacing in parishes all over the country.

'While some reactionary fringe groups have contrived to portray our association as a small coterie of radical priests with a radical agenda, we have protested vehemently against that unfair depiction. We are and we wish to remain at the very heart of the Church, committed to putting into place the reforms of the Second Vatican Council.

'Accordingly we wish to register our extreme unease and disquiet at the present development, not least the secrecy surrounding such interventions and the questions about due process and freedom of conscience that such interventions surface. At this critical juncture in our history, the ACP believes that this form of intervention – what Archbishop Diarmuid Martin recently called "heresy-hunting" – is of no service to the Irish Catholic Church and may have the unintended effect of exacerbating a growing perception of a significant "disconnect" between the Irish Church and Rome.'

This was a very strong statement from the leadership of the ACP and it was received positively by the members and by a large majority of Irish Catholics. There were objecting voices from some groups who see adherence to the teaching *Magisterium* of the Church as the only valid criterion but they did not receive great attention. Obviously the statement was noticed in the Vatican, because about six weeks later (some time in May, even though there was a June date on the document), an extraordinary response came from the CDF. The manner in which the response was delivered was even more curious and revealing than the content. It was handed to Brendan Hoban (one of the co-leaders of the ACP) by the Bishop of Killala, who said that the document came via the Papal Nuncio. Inside a blank envelope was an A4 page, not particularly well typed or presented, without any official heading, stamp or signature. We could only be sure that the document came from Cardinal Levada because Michael Brehl told me that he also received a copy by post from the cardinal. Its contents were as follows:

'CDF response to ACP regarding Fr Tony Flannery (11 June 2011)

'The Congregation for the Doctrine of the Faith (CDF) received belated notice of a declaration made by the Association of Catholic Priests (ACP) in Ireland which expresses its confidence in and solidarity with Fr Tony Flannery, CSsR, one of the ACP founding members.

'We noted with gratitude that the ACP says it does not espouse "a radical agenda", having as its purpose a commitment to "put into place the reforms of the Second Vatican Council". Nevertheless we could not ignore the mistaken notions contained in the ACP declaration about the CDF actions taken in regard to Fr Flannery. These actions were directed at Fr Flannery's public assertions in several of his columns in the magazine *Reality*, in which he expressed heretical or heterodox statements about central doctrines of the Catholic Christian faith.

'In his July/August 2010 article in *Reality*, for example, Fr Flannery made the following assertions:

'"I no longer believe that the priesthood, as we currently have it in the Church, originated with Jesus."

'"To say that at the Last Supper Jesus instituted the priesthood as we have it is stretching the reality of what happened."

'"I can no longer accept that interpreting the Word of God and celebrating the sacraments belong exclusively to the priesthood."

'The CDF brought these serious matters to the attention of Fr Flannery's superior general and proposed that he provide a program of study and prayer for Fr Flannery, away from the pressures of ordinary priestly ministry and with the guidance of a theologically well-instructed fellow priest, in order to allow him the necessary reflection to correct his heterodox views and to embrace the Catholic faith in its full truth and beauty. Such a period of reflection and correction would necessarily require Fr Flannery to step aside from giving parish missions, writing articles and participating in leadership of the ACP, since a priest's ministry presupposes his full profession of the Catholic faith that comes to us from the Apostles.

'The Church's canon law (*c.* 1044) calls a priest who has committed the delict of heresy "irregular for the exercise of orders received", while canon 1364 says that "a heretic…incurs a *latae sententiae* [sentence already passed] excommunication.' Before imposing the sanctions provided for in the law, it is the practice of the CDF to take steps to restore a priest to the faith and to ensure that he is not in a state of contumacy regarding the position(s) he may have taken.

'Only should these remedies fail would the canonical penalties be required. The CDF does not act "secretly" but through legitimate channels – in this case Fr Flannery's superior general – in order to protect a priest's reputation where public notice may not be required. In the present situation, the incorrect and even malicious interpretations given to the CDF's work on behalf of safeguarding the doctrine of the faith, that have appeared in the ACP declaration and in other media reports, require this present clarification.'

What was really remarkable was that this document contained very serious content – not least the threat of excommunication – but was not on headed notepaper and lacked a signature. It is hard to imagine any other institution acting in this way. I wonder who wrote the document and at what level it was, in a manner of speaking, signed off. Its main effect was to add some clarity to where I stood. If I did not get back in line and purge myself of what they called my 'heresies' I would run a serious risk of being excommunicated.

It would seem that someone in the Vatican realised that sending this document was not the brightest thing the CDF had ever done. Shortly after I received it I got a phone call from Michael Brehl appealing to me to speak to my co-leaders in the ACP to make sure that it was not made public. At that stage, as I was still abiding by the terms of what had been agreed, there was no danger that I was going to publish it.

Later on in that month of May 2012 Michael Brehl came to Ireland to discuss the situation with the governing council of the Irish Redemptorists. There is some suggestion that the general government of the Redemptorists disapproved of those colleagues who had spoken publicly in support of me and it is possible that this visit by the superior general was an effort to calm the situation, to see if it were possible to rein in my more outspoken colleagues. Given that the horse had already bolted, it was a bit late for injunctions to secrecy. Instead, reference was made to terms such as 'discretion' and the policy seemed to be that any public statement on the matter should be made by the relevant superiors.

After this the provincial leader, Michael Kelleher, held meetings in all the Redemptorist communities in order to keep the confrères (our term for fellow Redemptorists) informed. While I welcomed this at the time, later developments led me to suspect that this round of visitation was also an effort to keep a lid on the situation. I met Fr Brehl while he was in Ireland. Since things were progressing reasonably well at this point we had a pleasant and friendly chat, with nothing contentious about it.

The main thing I remember from this meeting was his reaction when I jokingly referred to the rumour that I had written Enda Kenny's famous speech in the Irish Dáil criticising the Vatican. He immediately said: 'And did you?' When I assured him I had nothing to do with it he breathed a deep sigh of relief. He told me that he had worried about it but decided not to ask me, so that if the people in the CDF questioned him about it he could genuinely say that he did not know. Now he was in a position to assure them that I had no connection whatsoever with the speech. The fact that some people in high positions believed rumours like this was an indication to me of how crazy the whole thing was becoming and also gave me a sense of the gullibility of some of the people in positions of power in the Church.

During my time of reflection I was in regular contact with Michael Brehl and invariably the subject of our discussion was how I might do enough to satisfy the CDF and be allowed back into priestly ministry. It had been mentioned before and now it emerged clearly that this body required a statement from me, a statement of faith on the contentious issues, which would be published in *Reality* magazine. Obviously they wanted me to recant and the 'statement' would confirm to the Vatican and to the public who had been 'misled' and 'confused' by my views that I had purged my heretical thinking and was now once again '*sentire cum Ecclesia*'. I was very uneasy about this but since the issues in dispute were mostly around questions about the origins of Church and priesthood, it didn't seem to me that there was sufficient reason to refuse. The upshot was that some of my time of reflection was taken up with drafting a statement that would be acceptable to the CDF, while not shattering my own integrity.

By the end of May, my period of reflection was coming to a conclusion. At the request of Michael Brehl and his deputy I went back to Rome to meet them, again accompanied by my brother Frank. While we were there I learned that things had taken a turn for the worse. Michael Brehl informed us that he had received what he described as 'a very angry letter' from Cardinal Levada. (We didn't, of course, get to see it.) Apparently he was angry over three things in particular. Firstly that the CDF dealings with me had gone public – of course they blamed me for that, although I had a strong suspicion that the leaks had come from the Vatican itself. Secondly he was angry that I had continued to be involved with the ACP during my time of reflection and had attended meetings. Reference to my attendance at an ACP meeting in Cork had appeared on the association's website. (This was my first clear indication that the website of the ACP was being carefully monitored in the Vatican.) Thirdly he was angry that other Redemptorists had come out publicly in support of me and he was demanding that they be disciplined. Clearly things were not going according to plan from his perspective. The Eucharistic Congress was shortly to be held in Dublin and the negative publicity the Vatican was getting was hardly an ideal preparation for the big event. Cardinal Levada wanted the whip cracked and people to be brought back into line.

What was most noticeable at this meeting was that Michael Brehl was under pressure. Enrique Lopez was more forthcoming, telling me that they were worried that there would be a revolt among the Irish Redemptorists. 'You might think,' he said to me, 'that you are the person most under pressure here. But you are not.' And he pointed over to the superior general. This was a plea to me to behave responsibly and get everyone off the hook.

At this meeting I came to a deeper realisation that whatever decisions I made would affect not just myself and those close to me but the Redemptorists in Ireland and around the world. I also had to consider the impact my decisions would have on the Association of Catholic Priests – but I had already given a good bit of thought to this. I believed that if I just walked away by resigning from the congregation, either going quietly or fighting my corner from outside, it would make life much easier for those in charge. I would become just one more name in the long list of priests who had re-signed from ministry. If I stayed and fought the battle from the inside it would be much more troublesome for the congregation. I got some good advice on this from one of my colleagues, who rejected any suggestion that I should just walk away, saying that the issues at stake were far bigger than me and that the Irish Redemptorists needed to work their way through them too, that they should not easily be let off the hook.

Having spent months immersed in this situation, I was really feeling the oppression of it all. I was weary of the uncertainty, of the efforts at resolution, of the cloud that was hanging over me. I left Rome the morning after that meeting, hoping that I would never see the place again.

12

Preparing a Statement

Meanwhile, my efforts at drafting a statement that could be published in *Reality* continued. I had no energy at all for the task so one of my colleagues, who is a theologian and who knew the Vatican scene much better than me, was crafting it for me. I was very grateful to him but my heart was definitely not in it and as a result the statement I ended up with was not really mine at all. It was written in a very different style and language from those I would use and was clearly designed to impress the people in the CDF.

Privately I knew I was playing the Vatican game and I was not pleased with myself for doing so and although I had agreed to produce the statement I was holding back on its publication in *Reality*. During this time I had several conversations with myself. On the one hand I judged that if this was what was required to get me off this particular hook, I was willing to do it. It didn't seem worthwhile to risk my priesthood for the sort of issues that were in dispute. I tried not to think too much about it and the fact that the statement was largely written by somebody else made it easier almost to pretend to myself that it wasn't happening, or that somehow it didn't involve me very much.

I would never have regarded myself as particularly holy or religious but my work as a preacher meant that the life and teaching of Jesus Christ had never been too far from my mind down through the years. My main difficulty with the situation in which I now found myself was that I could not see how it related in any way to the Gospel message. Even though my contact with the Vatican and its ways of doing business had at all times been at one remove, it began to have a deep impact on my perception of the whole

Church as an institution. Looking back I can see that I had never really been much of an 'institution person' but now I was becoming more alienated than ever. I often thought about the message I had received about waiting to see who I would be when this thing was done to me. I was facing up to the fact that this sequence of events would change me and all change involves loss. I was becoming a different person and was apprehensive as to how my future would unfold. But when I mentioned this to Michael Brehl, during our May meeting in Rome, he quickly dismissed it and assured me I would be the same person, in no way changed.

June is the month when the novena to Our Mother of Perpetual Help is held in many Redemptorist churches, the principal centres being Limerick, Esker and Belfast. I had been scheduled to preach in our church in Esker and, given that my period of reflection was at an end, I decided that I would preach at the event unless I got a written *diktat* prohibiting me from doing so. Just in case of any last-minute hitches I had discussed my decision with Michael Brehl when I visited Rome the previous month. He had no objection but recommended caution in the content of my sermons. I recall him advising me to preach as if Cardinal Levada or one of the other members of the CDF were sitting in the front seat. Considering that Esker is in a rural part of the west of Ireland it was mildly amusing to imagine this scenario.

The novena was a big event, with six sessions each day. I was born and reared within shouting distance of the monastery in Esker and had worked on this novena many times, so I knew a great number of the people who were attending and they were equally familiar with me. I preached at all the sessions on the first day and got a very warm reception. It was good to be back and I realised how much I had missed the work and the engagement with the people. I didn't exactly visualise Cardinal Levada in the front seat as Fr Brehl had advised me to do and without being in any way provocative, I got on with the work in my normal fashion and with a sense of gratitude that my life was returning to its usual pattern. On my last day of preaching I did allow myself a little bit of devilment. While promoting a new history of the Irish Redemptorists, covering the period from their coming to Ireland up to 2011, I quipped that it was a pity the author didn't continue to 2012, as I might have got a chapter in the book. This provoked great hilarity in the church. I don't know if it was reported to the CDF!

During the same month, June 2012, the Eucharistic Congress took place in Ireland. A great deal of preparation had gone into this event and there was an expectation among some that it would signal the beginnings of a resurgence in the Irish Church, or at the very least that it would be a turning point and we could begin to leave the difficulties of the previous twenty years behind us.

I think it is fair to say that publicity about the censoring of priests over the previous two months didn't help the build-up to the congress. It was reasonably successful, with good crowds attending the various events, but it was low-key and didn't have much of an impact, which was to be expected, given the climate in Ireland. The previous Eucharistic Congress that was held in Ireland had taken place in 1932 and still had a strong place in folk memory. In particular the famous Irish tenor, John McCormack, singing 'Panis Angelicus' at the final Mass in the Phoenix Park, attended by more than a million people, was an occasion not to be forgotten by those who witnessed it. The recording is still regularly played. The 2012 event made nothing of the same impression and certainly didn't bring about the type of resurgence of faith that some hoped for. The problems in the Irish Church are much too deep-seated to be solved by any one event, no matter how many ecclesiastical dignitaries are in attendance.

It is possible that my assessment was influenced by my experience of the institutional Church, as I felt alienated from the event and associated the foreign dignitaries who attended with the oppressive power that I had so recently encountered. Nor was my mood helped by meeting a nun who was visiting from the United States to attend the congress, who told me that she was praying for 'a good president' – and she did not mean Barack Obama.

Before the novena began I sent my statement to Michael Brehl because he was due to meet Cardinal Levada around 25 June. The plan was that it would be published in the September issue of *Reality*, although I was still withholding my consent to this part of it. I was not totally comfortable with any element of the process but I cooperated with it because there didn't seem to be anything that was worth making a stand on that might involve permanent dismissal from the priesthood. I was well aware that issues around the origins of the Church and the priesthood were more complex than my statement suggested and that they needed to be put in the context of our knowledge of the development of the early Church. But I considered that it was best to keep things simple: if this statement satisfied the CDF and got it off my back, it would be worthwhile.

The statement read:

'Since some concerns have been raised by the Congregation for the Doctrine of the Faith over possible interpretations of articles I have written in the past few years. I respectfully take this opportunity to clarify my views and to offer the reassurance necessary to lay those concerns fully to rest. Such words as I have written were written in good faith with absolutely no intent whatever to imply anything contrary to the truths we are all obliged to hold by the divine and Catholic faith to which I fully adhere and to which I have always adhered.

'I believe and accept that the Eucharist was given to us by Christ Himself; that in the Eucharist we receive "the Bread of Life", which is "the food of eternal life". I not only believe and accept this; over nearly forty years of ministry I have come to know the reality of it through my faith experience and I have been privileged to offer witness to it through my priestly ministry.

'I believe and accept that the Eucharist cannot be celebrated without a validly ordained minister.

'I believe and accept that the origins of the Eucharist and the priesthood can be found in the Last Supper, where, as Sacred Scripture tell us, Jesus gave the command to the apostles gathered around the table to "Do this in memory of Me".

'I believe and accept that the call to priesthood, indeed to all our Church's ministries, comes from God through Jesus Christ.

'I believe and accept that the Church has both the right and the duty to teach and preach the good news of salvation as promised by Jesus Christ and that we are reminded of this mission in the teachings of the Second Vatican Council. The decree on the Church's missionary activity tells us that the Church strives to preach the Gospel to all men and that it is the duty of the successors of the apostles to carry on this work (cf: *Ad Gentes*).

'It is my hope that the clarity and intent of this letter will be accepted in full satisfaction of the queries raised.'

Even though I was immersed in my preaching at the Esker novena and enjoying it, I was aware that tension was building in the upper echelons of the Redemptorists over the forthcoming meeting with Cardinal Levada. I received an email from Michael Brehl on 22 June which brought this into sharp focus. He thanked me for my statement and said how important it was that he had it for the meeting, about which he was clearly worried: 'I have to do some serious thinking and planning about how to approach the meeting with the CDF.' I was aware that the Irish provincial was in Rome at the time and I presume he was helping the superior general to prepare for the meeting.

At this point I was still holding back on publishing the statement. It seemed to me that this was a blatant attempt by the CDF to get me to grovel publicly and to destroy my credibility. On this subject Michael Brehl emailed me:

'I have asked you to reconsider your position that you will not publish a statement approved by them. If it is not this statement which you wrote for their eyes only, then would you consider writing an article based on this statement. After the widespread public nature of the coverage recently in the press (in April especially), they are insisting on a public clarification of what you believe. Please consider is there a way you can do this.'

He also reminded me that the CDF was asking for a longer period of spiritual and theological renewal. Clearly the people there believed that I had not yet come around to seeing things with their eyes!

The next part of Michael Brehl's email was particularly interesting. 'They want to know future plans for you and public ministry,' he wrote. And he added that unless I agreed to publish the statement: '...they will require you to engage in a longer period of reflection – with no public ministry. I do not know if they will impose restrictions on you, or if they will require the Redemptorists to do so.'

I was reminded of the judgement I had made when I first visited Rome back in February: that the Redemptorists authorities didn't see themselves as having any real power in this situation. They had to do what the CDF told them to do. In my eyes this made of Michael Brehl, amiable and well-meaning though he was, little more than a messenger for the Vatican. The email continued:

'I know that we will need to talk about your involvement with the Association of Catholic Priests. You realise that the question of resigning from the leadership was suspended pending this conversation. This will be a subject of the conversation on Monday, I have no doubt.'

I had suspected from the very beginning that this was the nub of the problem as far as the Vatican was concerned. I believe that they thought that if they could dismantle the leadership of the ACP they would be on the road to undermining the association. If they could sideline the current leadership they would frighten off any others who might take our place and in this way crush the whole movement.

In the last part of the email, consciously or unconsciously, Brehl piled on the pressure: 'They want to know the plans of the Redemptorists to address the harm caused by the public scandal – by the leaks of the requirements and by comments made by other Redemptorists.' There had indeed been a public scandal but for them the cause of the scandal was the 'leaking' of their dealings with me, which shows how far out of touch with reality they were. The real scandal was their behaviour. Although I was not responsible for bringing this behaviour out in the open, I did not regret that it had happened and I still believe that it is important to let people know the methods they were using in this investigation and their lack of justice and fairness. It is for this reason that I am writing this book.

I can clearly remember receiving this email from Michael Brehl. I was preaching at all the sessions of the novena that day and his email was a very unwelcome message in the midst of this. I particularly remember a sense of things closing in around me, a feeling that no matter what I did I would never be free of the CDF, that I would never again have the freedom to speak my mind but would always be looking over my shoulder. It was becoming clearer to me that I would soon have to make a major decision about my life.

Before the meeting between Michael Brehl and Cardinal Levada, after much thought and despite considerable reservations, I agreed that my statement could be published. Michael Brehl was happy to hear this, as presumably it strengthened his hand at the meeting with Levada which took place on Monday 25 June. I had warned Michael that I would be preaching all that day and that I would appreciate if he did not email me until the following day. But I did get an email from him that evening, which contained the following:

'The meeting went much better than we expected – certainly much better than I expected. We began with the statement that you sent me. Cardinal Levada asked me to read it aloud to him. When I finished he said, "That is a very fine declaration." I asked him if I could tell you that. He said yes but also added that they need to study it a little more and then respond in writing. So he did qualify it but he also told me I could tell you that. I think you have dealt successfully with the heresy charge. This moves things into a different arena.'

A phone call the following day confirmed that his worst fears about the meeting had not been realised. The anger that Cardinal Levada had displayed in his letter of two weeks previously (relating to the fact that matters had become public) seemed to have dissipated. The statement was acceptable, possibly with some minor amendments. There was no talk of any further periods of 'reflection' and the issue of the public support of the other Redemptorists was easily dealt with by Michael Brehl's assurance to Cardinal Levada that the Irish provincial had talked to these men and that this type of action would not be repeated. Nor did my position in the ACP come up for discussion. Michael Brehl's interpretation was that, as it cleared up the matter of heresy, my statement also put an end to the threat of excommunication that had come in the earlier document. (As things developed and a further statement was demanded, I believed the threat of excommunication remained.) It seemed as if the matter could now fairly easily be put to bed and that we could get on with our lives.

This all amounted to a big change in tune by the CDF. The people who knew about this development, particularly those who were veteran 'Vatican watchers', had a great time speculating about what might have happened to bring about this sudden change. From the beginning my brother and I had impressed on the Redemptorist superiors the need to warn the CDF that if they continued with their original course of action it could have a serious impact on the Irish Church. More by accident than design I and the other censored priests had become something of a symbol of the repression of free speech and of all that was wrong with the government of the Church. Maybe this message had got through. Maybe the CDF had decided that this was more trouble than it was worth and that the sensible thing to do was to put it quietly aside. Some people concluded that one or other of the senior clerics who were in Ireland for the congress had brought this message back to Rome.

We expected a written response to my statement from the CDF fairly soon, noting the amendments they required in order to facilitate the publication of the statement in the September 2012 issue of *Reality*. But nothing came. And then we heard that Cardinal Levada, having reached the specified age, had retired. About a month later his successor, Gerhard Müller, a German archbishop, was announced. There was intense speculation in the media, especially the Catholic papers, about this new man, as his past career seemed to give contradictory signals. While he was known to be very opposed to the Austrian Priests' Initiative (along the lines of the Irish ACP) he was a friend of the liberation theologian, Gustavo Gutierrez; they had even co-authored a book on liberation theology. None of the commentators were too sure what he would be like as head of the CDF.

I wasn't particularly worried, because I understood that the matter of my alleged 'heretical' thinking had been resolved by Cardinal Levada's acceptance of my statement and that it would not be raised again by the new incumbent. I should have remembered a conversation I had with Michael Brehl and Enrique Lopez, during which they suggested that some of Cardinal Levada's assistants were much more hardline than their line manager.

13

Archbishop Müller Ups the Ante

Summer is the easiest time of year for Redemptorist priests, as we take a break from preaching missions and novenas during July and August. In the summer of 2012, I was glad to relax after the tension of the previous few months. The time passed quietly and I began to distance myself from the whole episode, convincing myself that the trouble was over.

A phone call from Michael Brehl on 6 September put paid to this hope. He had received a communication from the CDF, clearly a serious one, but he would not tell me what it contained. Instead he wanted me to come out to Rome, for the third time, at the earliest possible opportunity. This was Thursday and he suggested that I would come the following Sunday. To be fair to him, he could not have been aware that 9 September was the day of the All-Ireland hurling final, in which my own county, Galway, was playing! For me the match was certainly going to get priority but apart from this I was reluctant to drop everything yet again and rush out to Rome. I said I would get back to him and when I had time to think about it I emailed him back:

'Dear Michael

'I am responding to your phone call of Thursday, 6 September informing me of the latest communication from the CDF and requesting me to come to Rome to meet with you.

'I understand from your call that this communication is looking for further changes to my statement and possibly other things of which I am not aware.

'I believe it is important for me to have either a copy of the communication, or to be acquainted with the substance of what precisely is being sought, before we meet. That would give me time to seriously consider these new developments, to consult with those close to me and in that way to be ready for a fruitful conversation with you.

'Our first meeting, where I was presented with two documents of enormous import and which we then proceeded to discuss, was not satisfactory from my point of view. I had no time to reflect calmly on the documents and as such I was at a disadvantage in the discussion. I know that I did not make you aware of my feelings at the time but I also know that I do not wish that to happen again.

'So I request that you find some way of communicating this document to me and then, at a time suitable for all of us, Frank and I will be happy to go to Rome and discuss the content with you.'

Michael Brehl phoned me back and gave me the substance of the latest communication. The new head of the CDF, Archbishop Müller, was demanding four further inserts into the statement that I had prepared. There were also two 'instructions'. Michael Brehl was willing to send over the document containing the four inserts but he would not send me the 'instructions' in writing. As I understood them from our telephone conversation, the instructions were as follows:

Firstly, I was to take a more extended period of 'spiritual and theological reflection'. This was 'ideally' to happen in a retreat house outside Ireland. I was to remain there until such time as the CDF approved of the statement. Once again I was to be taken out of public ministry, a situation that would last until the statement was approved. I would have to promise to have no contact with media and not to publish anything during this period.

Secondly, I was immediately to cease all involvement 'both public and private' with the Association of Catholic Priests and to have no further involvement until such time as the statement was published.

It is important to note that the CDF was ordering Michael Brehl to give me these instructions, because spokespeople for the Vatican have often claimed that matters to do with the disciplining of religious is solely the responsibility of the relevant religious superiors. In my experience, this was clearly not the case.

The upshot of the instructions was that I was to be indefinitely silenced and removed from ministry.

Up to this point, in my dealings with Michael Brehl, I had largely been compliant and willing to go along with the process. But I lost my patience during this phone call. I told him that it was disgraceful and intolerable that I was not being given these instructions from the CDF in writing. People were imposing *diktats* on me that were having a serious impact on my life: they were even ordering me to leave my country and stay away until they gave me permission to return. But they communicated these *diktats* to me by phone, with nothing on paper.

I was aware that Michael Brehl was under pressure and eventually he admitted that the CDF did not want me to have these instructions in writing. I would be given the four inserts, although he would neither post nor email them to me. He explained that a man was shortly travelling from Rome to Belfast who would bring the document and I was to arrange how it would travel from Belfast to me in the west of Ireland. I presume this had all to do with some extreme notion of secrecy but it sounded more like a 'B' version of a James Bond film. When the communication arrived the envelope contained just one page; as expected, there was no second page with a list of the sanctions to be imposed on me. However the four inserts were enough to give me plenty of food for thought. Once again, this communication from the CDF came on a plain A4 page, without stamp or signature. This is what was written on the page:

'Necessary Amendments to the Statement of Reverend Tony Flannery CSsR

'The following additions should be incorporated by Fr Flannery in his statement, which is the basis of the article of clarification that he intends to publish:

1. Regarding the Church, Fr Flannery should add to his article that he believes that Christ instituted the Church with a permanent hierarchical structure. Specifically, Fr Flannery should state that he accepts the teaching of the Second Vatican Council, as found in *Lumen Gentium* n. 9-22, that the bishops are the divinely established successors of the apostles who were appointed by Christ; that, aided by the Holy Spirit, they exercise legitimate power to sanctify, teach and govern the people of God; that they constitute one episcopal college together with the Roman Pontiff; and that in virtue of his office, the Roman Pontiff has full, supreme and universal power over the Church, which he is always free to exercise.

2. Regarding the Eucharist, Fr Flannery should add to his article that he believes that Christ instituted the priesthood at the Last Supper; that in the Eucharist, under the forms of bread and wine, the whole Christ is truly, really and substantially contained; that the Eucharist is a sacrifice because it re-presents (makes present) the sacrifice of the cross; and that only validly ordained priests can validly celebrate the Eucharist.

3. Regarding his statement concerning the priesthood, Fr Flannery should add to his article that he accepts that the Lord Jesus chose men (viri) to form the college of the twelve apostles and that the apostles did the same when they chose collaborators to succeed them in their ministry; and that the Church recognises herself to be bound by this choice made by the Lord himself and for this reason the ordination of women is not possible.

4. Furthermore, Fr Flannery should state that he accepts the whole teaching of the Church, also in regard to moral issues.'

I remember how angry I was during the phone call on 6 September. I considered that I was being bullied, both by the CDF and by

Michael Brehl. Rather than being interested in some form of compromise or negotiated solution, this new man in the CDF was clearly using the heavy hand of authority. He had introduced two issues into the statement, neither of which was there in the first place, except possibly by implication – the ordination of women and the teaching of the Church on moral issues. I had written on these topics and my views were well known but they weren't part of the original complaint against me.

My understanding is that either Archbishop Müller or one of those working under him was deliberately and calculatingly setting a trap for me. If I did not sign up to these new additions to the statement it seemed likely that I would come under *latae sententiae* excommunication. If I did sign, I would be contradicting what I had been saying for many years. Apart from the fact that in putting my name to this new statement I would be telling lies, I would lose all credibility. The part of the second instruction that seemed to say that I could return to my work with the ACP after the statement had been published made me laugh, though in an ironic rather that amused way. If I publicly put my name to that statement I would not be able to raise my head in public again, never mind continuing in leadership of the ACP. This, I presume, was the whole point of the exercise designed by the CDF. 'Not very nice people in that institution,' as a friend said to me.

Apparently the justification used by the CDF for introducing the last two items was that in earlier publicity some media suggested that these were the original complaints against me. Even though this was incorrect, the Vatican believed I was causing 'scandal' and 'leading people astray' in these areas and that this must be publicly corrected.

In some ways this latest document from the CDF was easier to deal with than what had gone before. Up to this point there was a lot of uncertainty, which had lead to my having endless conversations with myself, raising questions to which I couldn't formulate any definitive answers. How far would I go to meet their demands? What would I put into the statement that would be published in my name? Would I, like some other priests who had been censored, have to accept a situation where someone would be monitoring everything I said or wrote in the future? In sum, how much was I willing to put up with for the sake of continuing in ministry?

Some people suggested to me that there was a great amount of good I could still do as a priest and that I should not turn my back on this no matter what was foisted on me. They told me that any restriction was a small price to pay for the privilege of celebrating Mass and the sacraments, of preaching the Word of God and of bringing comfort to the sick and the dying. Their arguments had a degree of persuasiveness that left me wavering all through the spring and early summer. Not only were my mind and my thoughts wavering, my moods were fluctuating. Some days I was upbeat and ready for what was to come, almost relishing the battle. But at other times I was very down, worried and frightened about what lay ahead and about my future. Where would I live if I were expelled from the priesthood and the congregation? How would I support myself? And after almost fifty years of living in community, how would I cope with the loneliness of old age by myself?

But now matters were much less ambiguous. There was no way I could do what they asked and still live with myself. All I had read and studied over the years about the question of women in the Church had convinced me that there was no theological or scriptural argument sufficiently persuasive to justify the position the Church has taken on this serious issue. Given the history of misogyny that has been so evident down through the centuries, I firmly believed that latent misogyny was behind many of the Catholic Church's arguments against the ordination of women. So if the CDF was making acceptance of its prohibition for all time of the ordination of women to priesthood a condition of my continuing in ministry, I did not see that I had any choice. I honestly believe that if the same test were given to all Catholics, even priests, and if they were truthful in their answers, a great many of them would be as unable as I was to sign the document with which I had been presented.

A similar dilemma presented itself to me in relation to the moral teaching of the Church, as it was expressed in insert number four. I fully agreed with Cardinal Martini's statement of September 2012 'from the grave' that the Church was two hundred years behind the times, particularly in relation to some aspects of its teaching on sexuality. I had always held that *Humanae Vitae*, Pope Paul VI's 1967 encyclical on contraception, was a grave mistake. I also believe that what the Church has to say about marriage, sexual orientation and compulsory celibacy for the priesthood needs to be revised to take account of the greater understanding and different perception we have of relationships and human sexuality in the present day. A teaching that developed out of an understanding of sexuality and the human body some fifteen hundred years ago and that has scarcely altered since then is surely not adequate for the present time. This is not about changing fundamental Christian teaching, as some would suggest but, as the Vatican Council put it, 'responding to the signs of the times' and listening to the *sensus fidelium*, the voice of the people.

The Church has done this in other areas. Teaching on many aspects of life, for instance social justice and ecology, has changed and developed down through the years. But most aspects of its teaching on human sexuality have remained rigid and unbending. The result is that the Church has lost its voice in this important area of human life. A recent survey commissioned by the Association of Catholic Priests revealed that 75 per cent of practising Catholics in Ireland no longer find the Church's teaching on sexuality credible or relevant to their lives.

In September 2012 I found myself faced with a stark choice:

either agree to the new *diktats* or risk ministerial limbo. Some people advised me, with the best will in the world, to go to experts on theology and canon law, who would produce a statement that would satisfy the Vatican while leaving enough theological loopholes – in short, wriggle room – to enable me to put my name to it in conscience. They assured me that those 'in the know' who read it would understand what I was doing, citing examples of other priests, mostly theologians, who had done this and were able to continue in ministry.

My difficulty with this scenario was precisely that I was not a theologian. In preaching parish missions and novenas I constantly tried to present the Gospel message in a language that was intelligible and accessible to the ordinary person, who for the most part had not studied theology. I believed that if I now turned to the use of obscure language – open to different interpretations that might be obvious to theologians but certainly not to the average person in the pew – I would be betraying an important principle of my life's work. I would also in a real sense be deceiving the people who would read what I had written.

Despite this I was willing to make another effort to mollify the CDF. My colleague, who is better versed in the sort of language and argumentation that impresses the Vatican and who had helped me with the earlier statement, made an attempt to adapt it to the new demands and presented me with the results. When I read the revised version I knew that I could not, in conscience, put my name to it. So, after much consideration and a lot of discussion with my friends, I rejected this way of dealing with my situation.

14

Taking a Stand

While the latest communication from the CDF, although un-welcome, clarified some things for me and helped me to see the path I had to follow, it left me feeling very angry and disillusioned. The fact that the document was not headed, signed, or dated, which showed a total lack of respect for me as a human being, left me wondering what game was being played. Was there was a tactical reason behind it? In the event of my bringing all this into the public domain, would the CDF disown these documents?

In relation to censored priests from other religious congreg-ations I had seen how the CDF had tried to pass on all respon-sibility for disciplinary action to their superiors. When journalists questioned them the CDF would answer that they had nothing to do with such matters and that the journalists should approach the priest's own superiors. If this was the reasoning behind documents unsigned and on unheaded paper it showed a very low moral level but by this stage I would not have been surprised at anything that came out of the Vatican – a sad reflection on a body that purports to represent Christ on earth.

Anger tends to immobilise me. I knew I was not going to give the CDF the statement they were looking for and I intended not to respond at all. I considered that their mode of operation did not deserve the dignity of a response. Let them do their worst: I would survive. At this point one of my friends took me in hand and said that I must shake myself out of my lethargy and send a response. I objected that I hadn't any energy for the task and anyway what was there to say and what was the point, since it would make no difference. Instead of trying to persuade me further, she sat at her computer and began to frame a response to the four inserts. As a result, I had the outline of a statement that reflected my beliefs. I doubted that it would be well received but I could see that it was important for me to put my position in writing for the record and so that I could fulfil what was asked of me. My statement was not in theological language and did not use any technical or obscure terms. When I had finished working on my response I presented it at a meeting with two of my colleagues in the ACP and they helped me further to refine it. I was happy to put my name to it as it was a clear statement of where I stood:

Response to the Document Received from the Congregation for the Doctrine of the Faith on 13 September 2012

1. Regarding the Church, Fr Flannery should add to his article that he believes that Christ instituted the Church with a permanent hierarchical structure. Specifically, Fr Flannery should state that he accepts the teaching of the Second Vatican Council, as found in *Lumen Gentium* n. 9-22, that the bishops are the divinely established successors of the apostles who were appointed by Christ; that, aided by the Holy Spirit, they exercise legitimate power to sanctify, teach and govern the people of God; that they constitute one episcopal college together with the Roman Pontiff; and that in virtue of his office, the Roman Pontiff has full, supreme and universal power over the Church, which he is always free to exercise.

'I acknowledge and accept the teaching of the second Vatican Council. I have studied *Lumen Gentium* and it is clear from the teaching of the Council that the Lord Jesus set the Church on its course by preaching the Good News. The Council also accepts the teachings of the First Vatican Council, which declares that Jesus Christ, the eternal shepherd, established His holy Church, having sent forth the apostles as he himself had been sent by the Father; and he willed that their successors, namely the bishops, should be shepherds in His Church, even to the consummation of the world. The Council also teaches that Jesus placed Peter over the other apostles and instituted in him a permanent and visible source and foundation of unity of faith and communion. Vatican II states that "all this teaching about the institution, the perpetuity, the meaning and reason for the sacred primacy of the Roman Pontiff and of his infallible Magisterium, this sacred council again proposes to be firmly believed by all the faithful." I submit to this teaching in faith. I further accept the teaching of Vatican II that Jesus appointed twelve apostles and that he formed them into a stable group and that he placed Peter over them and that Peter was the chief cornerstone, the leader. I accept and believe that these apostles appointed successors and these successors appointed other successors of whom our present bishops are the apostolic successors. I believe that these bishops, by virtue of their episcopal consecration, inhabit the office of teaching and of governing in the Church. I also believe that this power to teach and govern can be exercised only in hierarchical communion with the head and members of the episcopal college. Again, in the context of all that the Council also taught about collegiality, I submit to it in faith. More than all of the above, I believe in Jesus Christ and that He, in His person, in His teaching and in His death and resurrection from the dead, is the source of salvation for the whole world.'

2. Regarding the Eucharist, Fr Flannery should add to his article that he believes that Christ instituted the priesthood at the Last Supper; that in the Eucharist, under the forms of bread and wine, the whole Christ is truly, really and substantially contained; that the Eucharist is a sacrifice because it re-presents (makes present) the sacrifice of the cross; and that only validly ordained priests can validly celebrate the Eucharist.

'I accept that the words of Sacred Scripture, "Do this in memory of Me", are inspired by the Holy Spirit. My understanding is that Scripture scholars tell us that the Gospels began as oral tradition and gradually the stories and teaching of Jesus were put into written form, first in the writings of St Paul and the *Acts of the Apostles* and later in the four Gospel accounts that have come down to us. These writings, which we believe are divinely inspired, tell us that very early, following the ascension of Christ into Heaven, His followers began to gather, to retell the stories and celebrate the meal, just as Jesus had done. They did this as He had requested and so what we now call the Eucharist became a central part of the life of the early community. Gradually they began to realise that when they shared the bread and the cup, Jesus was really present with them. And so I have no difficulty in believing that the origins of the Eucharist are to be found in the Scripture accounts of the Last Supper and that Jesus is really and truly present when we celebrate the Eucharist.

I believe that the priesthood, as we now know it, was not there from the beginning but developed gradually. The early Christian communities chose one of their group to preside at the celebration, while other members of the community took on other functions. Only gradually did these different functions come together in one person, who began to be termed "priest". Since the function of the Jewish priest was to offer sacrifice, the Christian priest also assumed the role of one who offered sacrifice to the Father, on behalf of the people. In saying this I am not suggesting that the development of priesthood in the early Church was not according to the mind of Christ. I accept the teaching of Vatican II that the ministerial priest, by the sacred power he enjoys, teaches and rules the priestly people; that the ministerial priest acts in the person of Christ when he makes present the Eucharistic sacrifice and offers it to God in the name of all the people.'

3. Regarding his statement concerning the priesthood, Fr Flannery should add to his article that he accepts that the Lord Jesus chose men (*viri*) to form the college of the twelve apostles and that the apostles did the same when they choose collaborators to succeed them in their ministry; and that the Church recognises

> herself to be bound by this choice made by the Lord himself and for this reason
> the ordination of women is not possible.

'I have always been impressed by the significant presence of women in the life of Jesus, as recounted in the Gospels, and the writing of St Paul and the *Acts of the Apostles* suggest that they were also significant in the early Church.

'I am also conscious of the work of the Pontifical Biblical Commission of 1976. Having studied the question, the commission voted unanimously that the New Testament does not settle in a clear way and, once and for all, the problem of the possible accession of women to the presbyterate. Secondly, the possibility that the scripture gave sufficient indications to exclude the ordination of women was defeated by a majority of seven votes. And finally the proposition that the Church hierarchy could admit women to ordination without going against Christ's original intentions was approved by the same majority.

'My years of pastoral ministry have informed me that many women find the current Church teaching on this matter very difficult. *Lumen Gentium* 12 states that: 'The entire body of the faithful, anointed as they are by the Holy One, cannot err in matters of belief. They manifest this special property by means of the whole people's supernatural discernment in matters of faith when "from the bishops down to the last of the lay faithful" they show universal agreement in matters of faith and morals. There are clear indications from research and also from my many years of pastoral experience that a great many of the faithful have not 'received' this teaching. Putting this together with the findings of the Pontifical Biblical Commission, I am left with serious questions about the teaching on the ordination of women in the Catholic Church. I also have questions as to whether sufficient level of discernment was undertaken prior to the decree that the topic of the admission of women to ministerial priesthood should not be discussed by faithful members of the Catholic Church. I have given this serious consideration and I find it difficult to dismiss the strong possibility that the Holy Spirit may have been speaking through the aforementioned Pontifical commission and may be currently speaking through the voice of the faithful. So I am left with serious and difficult questions.

'In this context, I point to the *Declaration on Religious Liberty* issued by Vatican II. This document states that human persons are bound to adhere to the truth, once they come to know it, and direct their whole lives in accordance with truth. I am aware that the thrust of the *Declaration on Religious Liberty* focuses on the religious freedom that must be accorded to the human person by the civil authorities. However, I believe when the Church declares "in religious matters, every form of coercion by men should be excluded". I think that this teaching should also guide the governance of the Church in dealing with its own members.'

4. Furthermore, Fr Flannery should state that he accepts the whole teaching of the Church, also in regard to moral issues.

'This part of the request from the Congregation for the Doctrine of the Faith seems to particularly focus on Church teaching on moral issues. As with my response to the last question, it is also clear to me that some matters of Church teaching on sexual issues are not "received" by the majority of faithful Catholics. Again this is shown by the results of research in various parts of the world and also clearly in my years of pastoral experience. So I am left with the same serious and difficult question. Is it possible that in this area also the spirit is speaking to us through the voice of the committed believers?

'I have worked for almost forty years as a Redemptorist priest, trying to follow the instruction of our founder, St Alphonsus, that I should have particular care for the most abandoned, for those on the margins of society or Church, and for those who feel lost and alone. In this context I have experienced difficulty also with the way in which Church moral teaching has been presented and imposed on people. I have always been very conscious of the warning of Jesus that we should not be like the Pharisees, placing impossible burdens on people's shoulders and not lifting a finger to help them. There have been times when teachings were imposed without the necessary degree of understanding and compassion. Of course we must strive for the ideal, as laid out in the Gospels, but, like Jesus, we must be compassionate, accepting and forgiving of the weakness and failure of humanity, including ourselves.

'Finally, may I say this about the dispute that exists between the Congregation for the Doctrine of the Faith and myself:

'I hope that I am a committed member of the Catholic Church and of the Congregation of the Most Holy Redeemer. I have spent my priestly life preaching the Gospel of Jesus Christ to the best of my ability. I believe that my life as a priest and religious has been a great privilege, one of which I am not worthy. I love the Catholic Church. Its spirituality has nourished me through my life. I don't want to belong to any other Church. I ask to be allowed to practise my priesthood. I see how His Holiness, Pope Benedict, has been able to reach out to the followers of Bishop Lefèbvre and such reconciliation bears witness to the Gospel of Jesus Christ. I ask that this inclusiveness also include me. In humility and charity, I point out that I have not made any public comments that have not been made by moral theologians and scripture scholars who are teaching in institutions that have the approval of the teaching Magisterium of the Holy Catholic Church. I cannot do otherwise than follow my conscience.

This is where I stand. This is my statement.'

Fr Tony Flannery CSsR

15

Misogyny in the Catholic Tradition

As the issue of women in the Church has now come to centre stage in this story I will pause in the next chapter and reflect on one of the really shameful aspects of Church history, which, I believe, still influences attitudes in the Church and its teaching. I refer to misogyny.

Hypatia of Alexandria is one of the few pagan woman philosophers whose name has come down to us, though not for reasons that I suspect she would have wished. She was born in Alexandria towards the end of the fourth century, the daughter of a mathematician. Commentators of the time say that she 'far surpassed all the philosophers of her own time': she taught Platonic and Aristotelian philosophy in both Athens and Alexandria and published many books. In her personal life she was something of an ascetic, although described as very beautiful.

The bishop of Alexandria at the time was Cyril, who was a fiery orator with a reputation for intolerance; he searched out 'heretics' with great zeal. Some Christian writers at the time began to mutter about Hypatia, most likely because of her influence on people's thinking, suggesting that she was a witch, under the control of the devil. Cyril preached one of his fiery sermons attacking her, which provoked a mob to descend on her academy. The mob dragged her to the church, stripped her naked and used oyster shells to tear off her skin. Then they burned her alive.

Cyril is now a saint and doctor of the Church, with a feast day on 28 January. He was one of the main proponents for having Mary declared mother of God at the Council of Ephesus in 431. I suggest that his involvement in the murder of Hypatia and the

declaration of Mary as the mother of God might not be as contradictory as first appears.

The terrible story of Hypatia is just one example of the history
of misogyny in the Christian Church. But misogyny had its origins
much earlier. The early Church was influenced in many ways by
Greek philosophy, especially by the great philosophers Plato
and Aristotle. It is interesting to note the close similarity between
the creation myths found in Greek and Jewish culture. We are
familiar with the Jewish/Christian myth as recounted in the *Book
of Genesis*. Adam (man) was created first and then Eve was created
out of Adam, as a companion and helpmate. But it was Eve who
succumbed to the temptations of the serpent and seduced Adam
into sin, thus bringing about what we know as the fall of man and
original sin. It was woman who brought hardship and death into
this world, she who spoiled paradise.

The Greek creation myth was first written down by Hesiod in
the 8th century BC. In this narrative men were created and put on
earth by the demi-god Prometheus. There were no women among
them and these companions to the gods had an existence similar
to the Garden of Eden, free from the destructive power of disease
and death. But the father of all the gods, Zeus, was jealous of these
men and, in order that they should not get above themselves and
challenge the gods, he deprived them of the secret of fire so that
they would have to eat their meat raw and thereby remain at the
same level as the other animals. Prometheus, sympathetic to his
creation, stole fire from heaven and brought it down to earth. Zeus
was furious at being deceived and in order to punish men he gave
them the gift of a woman, Pandora, referred to as the 'beautiful
evil'. Pandora married the son of Prometheus and became the
mother of all women. When she came to earth, she brought with
her a sealed, womb-shaped, jar which she had been strictly ordered
not to open. But she did open it and in this way she scattered pain
and evil among men.

The sexual symbolism of this is obvious and also the fact that in both creation myths the woman is the source of evil, suffering and death. Feminine beauty, attractiveness and sexuality are the trap that ensnare men. As St Augustine wrote in *The City of God*, referring to the fall of humanity in the Garden of Eden: 'From that moment, then, the flesh began to lust against the spirit. With this rebellion we are born, just as we are doomed to die and because of the first sin, to bear, in our members and vitiated nature, either the battle with or defeat by the flesh.'

Saint Augustine (354-430) is one of the most significant figures in Christian history. After an early life of debauchery, which he recounts in great detail in his *Confessions*, he converted to Catholicism under the influence of St Ambrose. He had already become a disciple of Greek philosophy, especially the work of Plato. Plato wrote about an ideal society which would be governed by men who lived what he termed the 'pure form', an existence detached from all physical desires and lusts. It was as a result of Augustine's intellectual brilliance as well as the emotional and psychological struggles that characterised his life that the great convergence of Greek philosophy and Christian/Jewish teaching happened, a convergence that has had enormous influence on Church teaching down to today.

This is from Jack Holland's *The History of Misogyny, The World's Oldest Prejudice*:

'The idea of "fall" had been inherited from the Jewish myth of the expulsion of man from the Garden of Eden. To this fall of man, Augustine adds another, even more terrible dimension: the Platonic fall. This is the fall from the pure form, to Christians the timeless perfection of union with God, into the mutable world full of life, lust, suffering and death. It comes about through conception. From that moment we are in a state of sin – original sin. As Augustine says, quoting the *Psalms*, we are "conceived in iniquity and in sin" in our mother's womb. The instrument of this fall from grace is woman; both in the sense that it was Eve's disobedience that led to our expulsion from paradise, and in the Platonic sense – she represents the wilfulness of the flesh to reproduce itself. We are thus carried away from God into temporal life in which we (thanks to our bodies) are in a state of rebellion against him. We will bring this fall upon ourselves, and our rebelliousness expresses itself most directly through sexual desire. Because of original sin man, who might have been spiritual in body, became carnal in mind.'

Out of this line of thinking came the whole notion of subduing the body and repressing sexual desire, with which those of us who grew up in Catholicism are familiar. To be fair to Augustine he had a more subtle and nuanced view of women than some other fathers of the Church. He did not see woman as inherently evil but as the beings who evoked lustful desire in the male. To quote again from Jack Holland:

'In *The City of God* he stresses that "the sex of woman is not a vice but nature". But the terrible anguish of his struggle with desire, which he records with such power, reveals clearly that it is man's battle with himself that is at the root of misogyny. As a punishment, God gave us sexual desire, something over which our will has no control. (The similarity with the Greek myth of Pandora is obvious here!) Just as we defied God, so our nature defies us. Sex became the battleground, both as a pleasure and a punishment, in a way unheard of before in western culture. Woman was bound to suffer because of our nasty habit of blaming that which we desire for making us desire it.'

In my understanding, this merging of Greek and Old Testament philosophy, mediated through Augustine, is of crucial importance in the history of the Church. It was man's struggle with his own desires and his inability to integrate and make peace with them that led to the latent hatred of women that has blighted Catholicism ever since. At its core, it wasn't women but their own nature that men were unable to come to terms with but it was women who were to suffer terribly as a result. The shameful history of the burning of women during the Middle Ages, instigated by the Church, makes for horrible reading. There is no definite record of how many women were burned at the stake in the period from the 14th to the 17th centuries but most estimates put it in the hundreds of thousands. These women were condemned by the Church as witches, accused of having had sexual relations with the Devil. They were judged and condemned by the Inquisition, the Vatican body that developed into the present-day Congregation for the Doctrine of the Faith. The Church handed these women over to the civil authorities to perform the executions. At that time, in many parts of Europe, the Church was so powerful that the civil authorities dared not refuse.

Some writers suggest that aspects of the teaching about Mary are the other side of the misogynist coin, presenting Mary as the virgin mother, the woman who was conceived without original sin, a person who never had sexual relations or experienced bodily passions or desires. Mary was elevated to the extent that she was no longer really human and, in some sense, the elevation of Mary has been used to control women in the area of sexuality.

A great tragedy for the Church is the fact that, as a result, the radical example of Jesus' behaviour towards women has largely been lost. His rejection of the culture and practice of his time in relation to women, his treatment of them as equals, are some of the most outstanding characteristics of his life and teaching. But the unhealthy combination of Greek and Jewish philosophy with the personal obsessions of Augustine served to bury this crucial part of the Gospel message. The current teachings in relation both to sexuality and the place of women in the Church are the legacy of centuries of misogyny.

The other tragedy is the fact that for two millennia the Church has largely deprived itself of the contribution women could make.

It would be difficult to calculate just how much good has been
denied the Church due to the sidelining of women down through
the ages. While women have formed the largest group of church
attendees, the faith and goodness of women have been left fallow
when it comes to Church teaching, policy and governance. They
could have added their intuitive wisdom of the mysteries of faith,
the teaching of Christ which was delivered in the presence of
women and the tradition and understanding of the Gospels.

It is just possible that a bit of female commonsense might have
prevented the recent, disastrous, introduction of the new missal.
I have met a number of women who thoroughly disapprove of
it and since the majority of Massgoers are women, it would have
been logical to get their views on the new text. Many people have
questioned whether the bungling response of the Church authorities to the clerical sexual abuse crisis would have been different if
women were in positions of influence in the Church or if priests
were married.

Historically women were largely left uneducated. Educated
women were feared and silenced by the Church because churchmen
saw women as evil, unreliable, fickle and servants of the devil. To
this day the Magisterium of the Church lacks the female intellect.
Many women therefore practised a religion of sentimental piety,
from which they got consolation and hope. But it was a poor sub-
stitute for the message of Jesus as found in the Scriptures which
they were not allowed to read. To this day a woman is not allowed to
read the Gospel at Mass – the Vatican still severely limits any public
role for women in the proclamation of the Word.

Clerical celibacy is not the topic of this book but I believe its
exalted position in the Catholic Church is another remnant of misogyny. When I headed out into the world as a young priest, with a
great deal of medieval philosophy, morality and dogma in my head,
I quickly discovered that in many ways lay people were far ahead
of me. The seminary training had isolated me too much from the

realities of life and from normal relationships with women and I had a lot to learn.

I met people who had long and often painful memories of sermons depicting an angry, exacting God. I suspect that the emotional excess of these sermons stemmed from suppressed sexuality. At Sunday Mass, when people should have been giving Eucharistic thanksgiving, they might be forced to hear their neighbour's daughter condemned as a 'fallen woman'. The lives of many people, particularly women, were forever blighted by such outbursts. One result of this was the creation of a climate of fear which had a detrimental effect on people's attitudes to sexuality and especially to women who had children outside marriage. (The same ignominy was not visited on the child's father.) We have to ask ourselves if the isolation and loneliness of the priest had anything to do with it. It is likely that living a normal life with a wife and children would have mitigated the harshness of some of the Sunday sermons. We still have compulsory celibacy in the priesthood and it is only fair to conclude that it is still doing a lot of damage to our humanity.

In my early years of seminary training there was something known as the 'great silence': total silence from night prayer in the evening until after morning Mass. But now I can see there was an even greater silence, relating to the vow of celibacy that we were taking on. We were a large group of young men, between the ages of eighteen and twenty-six, strong young men teeming with energy and all the normal sexual desires. Every week, riddled with guilt, we went to confession to old confessors and told them about our bad thoughts and imaginings. To be fair, they were kind men, who tended to encourage us and tell us that God would forgive us. Sexuality was not spoken about among the students, at least not in my hearing. Any talks we got on the subject were esoteric and idealistic. We were told that we should be able to divert our sexual energy into the search for intimacy with the Divine. Life has taught me that this is an unrealistic aspiration – and that is putting it mildly.

In 2011 Marie Keenan, a UCD sociologist, published the impressive book *Child Sexual Abuse and the Catholic Church: Gender, Power and Organisational Culture*. Keenan worked for more than twenty years both with survivors and perpetrators of sexual abuse and their families, in community and forensic settings. The book contains penetrating insights into the dark silence of the Church, including a deep analysis of the seminaries, exposing how the system stunted the maturity of the young men studying to be priests. It treats of the lack of warmth, of affection and of refinement in these houses of study. It points out the deprivation and negative effects of the lack of female presence and guidance. One passage from her book is particularly striking:

'Another question arises: is the aim of spiritual salvation worth the sexual sacrifice? Or are not the means and the ends totally out of synch for modern conditions? Is it not cruel to demand lifelong sexual abstention from human beings, despite all the research hinting at serious problems with such lifelong practices, especially when not voluntarily chosen? Against easily available scientific and social scientific knowledge and advice, the Church still continues to teach and train (how?) its clergy to abstain sexually. Knowing that such demands of sexual abstention are totally unrealistic, this is exactly where one aspect of institutional hypocrisy comes in as an explanation. The Church still promotes an institutional practice that is bound to fail. Cruelty and abuse are bound to arise from such impossible tasks. The power and control game (control men's bodies and you control their minds) has turned into a cynical exercise against better knowledge. Just for the purpose of order and maintaining the very institution, human lives are now sacrificed and destroyed, lives that include the identifiable victims of Catholic clergy, whose stories of pain resound around the world, but lives that also include the clergy themselves. Making celibacy mandatory for all Catholic clergy no longer serves anyone well. Celibacy must indeed be optional for individuals who wish to choose it, for reasons of belief, spirituality or faith, without the problems that accompany its mandatory companion.'

The Catholic Church in Ireland seems now to believe that it has dealt with the problems of clerical sexual abuse by putting structures in place to protect children. This is good. But no effort has been made to look at the deeper issues that led to the problem in the first place. There is still too much silence, there are still too many topics that cannot be discussed and the roots of the problem remain.

What I have written here is only scratching the surface of how the long tentacles of misogyny have reached down through the history of the Catholic Church and damaged the lives of men and women and how they have managed to blot out some of the most radical aspects of the message of Jesus. It would take a lot to convince me that somewhere in the inherited memory of those who insist on the celibacy of the clergy there is not still some echo of that ancient notion referred to earlier in this chapter that men deal with sacred things and that it would not be appropriate for them to have any dealings with women, who were seen as the origins of unruly desires and the gateway to evil. It is only when we face up honestly and courageously to the damage that misogyny has done to the Church and look again at how the teaching of the early Fathers was deeply influenced by their negative view of women that we can begin to rid the Church of this malevolence.

16

A Formal Precept of Obedience

In the third week in September, just as my native county Galway was revving up for another attempt to bring the McCarthy Cup across the Shannon, Michael Brehl returned to the CDF with my new statement. He was not taking the statement that the CDF demanded; it was a very different offering. I don't know how Michael Brehl felt about it. It is likely that he was as aware as I was that it would not be acceptable to them. I don't know what it is like for him and others in his position to approach these official Vatican bodies 'without the goods'. It is probable that they experience the degree of apprehension that we all feel when anticipating conflict. In my meetings with Michael Brehl I got a sense that he went across the Tiber somewhat 'cap in hand', as we might say in Ireland. I believe that in his dealings with Cardinal Levada he addressed him as 'Your Eminence'. In my view, if you address someone in this fashion, it immediately puts you at a disadvantage. You put yourself in the role of inferior addressing your superior, the balance of power is with the other person, and your position is considerably weakened. The best you can do is plead for leniency.

I was almost certain that there was no way the CDF were going to accept my statement. If they allowed me to continue in ministry while holding these views they would have to rescind actions they had taken against other priests and I knew they would not do this. They would not be able to admit publicly that they had made a mistake in their dealings with me. In presenting this statement I knew that, in all probability, I was signing my own order of exclusion from ministry for the rest of my life and that it would have other consequences, potentially even more serious.

I did not expect a quick response from the Vatican. My sense was that they had me where they wanted me – out of ministry, largely silenced and with my wings considerably clipped. I also believed that it would benefit them to play the long game: history shows they have a particular expertise in doing so. Despite this, in another corner of my mind I hoped that there was still a chance that there might be some little room for compromise. While this slight chance remained it would be hard for me to make the whole story public. If I did this, I would be the one who would effectively bring the negotiations, in so far as one could use that word to describe what had been happening, to an end.

On this occasion I misread the Vatican. Later on that same afternoon Michael Brehl phoned me to say that he had got a very decisive response from the CDF. The first thing he told me was that the CDF did not accept my statement, which was no great surprise. They described my statement as 'incomplete', something that really irritated me. It appears they had only one view of wholeness, something that encompassed their view and their view only. Michael Brehl told me that I was not to attend the AGM of the Association of Catholic Priests, which was scheduled for 9-10 November, two weeks later. He said that the CDF had instructed him, as my religious superior, to put me under a 'formal precept of obedience' not to attend.

I understood from him that he had been formally instructed by the CDF to do this. In other words, he had no say in the matter and the idea of banning me from attending the AGM of the Association of Catholic Priests did not originate with the Redemptorists. When I questioned him as to what would happen if I disobeyed this formal precept and attended the meeting, he acknowledged that it could lead to the initiation of the process of dismissal from the congregation. To emphasise this point he read out extracts from two of the constitutions of the congregation of the Most Holy Redeemer, the book of rules and regulations governing the life of Redemptorists. The first was part of Constitution 18:

'The task the congregation has assumed in the Church is in the service of Christ, and as a consequence, must also be in the service of the Church. Because their ministry is directed toward the good of the universal Church the members are primarily subject to the supreme pontiff, even by virtue of the vow of obedience.'

Even though I had lived for almost fifty years subject to these rules and constitutions I admit that I had never scrutinised them with great care. When I read this rule again after the phone call I noted how our constitution seemed automatically to assume that the service of Christ and the service of the Church were one and the same thing. At that stage of my life I could not readily accept this assumption and saw it as being dependent on the Church acting as the body of Christ on this earth and following His teachings.

The second extract Michael Brehl read out to me was from Constitution 73, Number 3:

'Lawful superiors can impose formal precepts of obedience on the members of their community concerning matters contained in the constitutions and statutes. Ordinarily, however, they should not use this power unless there is a grave reason and with the consent of their consultors. The members, because of the obedience they have professed before God, are bound to obey such precepts willingly and promptly.'

He emphasised the last phrase: that I should obey this precept 'willingly and promptly'. This conversation took place over the phone but it was clear that the situation had moved to a new level, and that, metaphorically speaking, we were entering really deep waters. I had known that it could come to this but had not expected it so quickly. When Michael Brehl said again that the consequence of my refusal to obey this formal precept could be dismissal from the congregation I asked him only one question: in the event of dismissal, would the congregation cease to have any responsibility for me. He replied that it would not. He then said that he would be sending me the formal precept in writing as soon as he could, so that I would receive it well before the date of the event in question. I found it interesting to hear that I would get this precept, although little else, in writing! Brehl strongly urged me to obey his orders, so as not to bring things to a head, leaving room for possible further negotiations. In my view the CDF had already done a very good job of bringing things to a head and I doubted whether Michael Brehl was himself holding out much hope of real and useful discussions taking place – if he was, he was not being very realistic.

He asked me to phone him within twenty-four hours, and said he hoped I would promise him not to attend the AGM. He said that he would still have to send the letter with the formal precept but he seemed to be anxious to get my promise, although I did not fully understand why. That telephone call really shook me and it took me a while to calm myself and be sufficiently coherent to consult with some of my friends, those who had supported me throughout this sorry series of events.

I reread the articles of our constitutions that Michael Brehl had quoted and quickly came to the conclusion that my attendance at the AGM of the Association of Catholic Priests was hardly a 'grave reason' justifying the issuing of a formal precept of obedience. I decided that I would not telephone back within twenty-four hours, as requested. It seemed to me that the request to phone him had more to do with his need than mine, something that became obvious when I got a call from him when the twenty four hours had barely elapsed. Having asked me how I was and assuring me that he was praying for me and presuming that I was also praying, he asked if I had anything to tell him.

By now relations between us were deteriorating and the informality and relative friendliness of our earlier exchanges were being replaced by a sharper and colder atmosphere. I said no, that I hadn't anything to say on the matter of attending the meeting. I said that

I would make up my own mind on the matter in my own time and that in the meantime I accepted that he had to do what he had to do. There wasn't much left to say so he assured me that he would be there for me if I wanted to talk to him, that I could just send an email and he would call back, no matter where he was.

To get a formal precept of obedience is about as serious as it can be for a member of a religious order. In all my years in the Redemptorists I had never heard of one being issued. Way back in my student days an old priest lectured us on the vow of obedience. He was a very intelligent man who, I suspect, had acquired a slightly cynical view of the whole notion after a lifetime's experience of its various manifestations. He spoke to us somewhat tongue in cheek about the different grades of obedience involved in the vow. 'And then,' he said, 'we come to the nuclear warhead, the formal precept of obedience.' He chuckled quietly and said no more So now the 'nuclear warhead' was being aimed at me and I wasn't laughing. I would either have to obey or run the very real risk of being dismissed from the congregation.

Inevitably I began to think back on the whole notion of obedience and my understanding of it.

I joined the Redemptorists at the age of seventeen. But that is not the full story. I am the youngest of a family of four, three boys and one girl. We grew up on a small farm in County Galway in the west of Ireland. Our mother was a primary school teacher but the law in Ireland at this time was that she had to give up teaching on getting married. Our father worked on the farm and for much of our upbringing he also worked for Bord na Móna on the local bog. Bord na Móna was a state company set up in the 1940s to develop the boglands of Ireland and provide fuel for the nation's fires and electricity generation stations. Dad worked on a machine called a loader, which filled the saved turf from the reeks into the wagons that transported it to the depot, where it was sold. It was an extremely dusty job. These Bord na Móna works are closed now but if this job were still in existence there would be numerous health and safety regulations about it. Although my father was only an occasional and light smoker, a lifetime of breathing turf dust condemned him to an early death from lung cancer. By now all of us, his children, have outlived his length of days.

My father never went beyond primary school and even there learned very little. He always used to tell us that he sat inside the back door – for whatever reason, the teacher seemed to think he was a poor prospect for learning. As a result, while he could read well and indeed was a voracious reader of newspapers, he never learned how to write beyond being able to sign his name and that only when he had to. Mother was the educated one in the house, so she looked after all the side of life that involved dealing with paperwork, making phone calls and writing letters. But my father was an intelligent man who took a great interest in politics, current affairs and the local community. He even had opinions on matters to do with religion, something that was not very common in an Ireland dominated by a very authoritarian Catholic Church. Looking back now I can see that he was a surprisingly free-thinking man for his time but he was by nature cautious and nervous, so his actions did not always measure up to his thought processes. I believe that his lack of education gave him an inferiority complex and the fact that his wife, our mother, was older than him perhaps meant that he tended to defer to her in most things.

He was a very good man and there is a lot I am sorry I did not say to him before he died. In our household we did not go in for physical affection and we would also have been embarrassed by any great verbal expressions of affection. He died after a short illness. It took some time for the diagnosis of lung cancer to be made, by which time the cancer had spread to other vital organs. We had no realisation of the seriousness of his illness. Up to the moment of the diagnosis we just thought that whatever was wrong with him could at least be managed and we did not consider his death to be a real and imminent possibility. He was frightened. This all happened thirty-three years ago but I still have the clearest image of the day we brought him into hospital – it must have when the final diagnosis was made – and he looked back at us as they wheeled him away on a wheelchair. I wish I had run across and thrown my arms around him and told him what a wonderful man and father he was. But we didn't do that sort of thing!

The death of a parent, especially the first parent, is a big event in most of our lives. But I recognise clearly now that my father's death brought about a change in me. I felt sad that his innate caution had held him back throughout his life and at some, almost unconscious level, I wanted to ensure that this would not happen to me. I was going to stand for what I believed and not let fear cripple me.

Our parents were ambitious for their children. They were determined that we would get an education, so that we wouldn't end up working in the bog or having to emigrate, which in the Ireland of the 1950s was the main option for young people. Since at the time there was no easy access to second level education for people living in the country and since we lived close to a Redemptorist monastery and attended Mass and devotions there regularly, it was decided that the boys in the family should go to the Redemptorist boarding school in Limerick. As boarding schools went at the time, this particular one was fairly civilised. There was little corporal punishment and the food was reasonably good. It was a small school of about a hundred pupils, so there was a fair degree of individual attention. The teachers were all Redemptorist priests. I was looking forward to going there, as my two brothers had gone ahead of me and I had heard many a good story about the place. It sounded glamorous and exciting for a young fellow living in the country in those times.

Looking back now I can see that the big disadvantage of the school was the fact that it was what was known then as a junior seminary. In other words, all the boys who attended this school were meant to be on the way to becoming Redemptorists. The notion of a twelve year old boy being set on course for the priesthood sounds preposterous today but was common at that time. So while the atmosphere of the school was quite civilised, there was a fair bit of what would now be termed brainwashing. There was very close monitoring of what we could read and the works of St Alphonsus and Thomas à Kempis were regularly read at common meals. This was heavy stuff for young fellows beginning out in life, laden down as it was with negativity and fear of eternal damnation. I don't know about other students but that heavy sense of the deadly seriousness of life and the huge consequences in the next life of the choices I made and the actions I took had a big impact on me.

In my youth I certainly did not experience religion as something that set me free. The notion of Jesus coming to give me the fullness of life never penetrated my consciousness in those teenage years. Not that I was particularly religious. In fact I would say I tended towards the opposite. I loved sport and played any game that was available to me. I wasn't very studious, just doing enough to get by. The conferences and retreats that were a regular part of life in the school I generally found dull and boring. The daily Mass at 6.30 in the morning was a duty rather than any sort of uplifting experience. The weekly confession was a ritual. I generally played fairly loose with the school rules but without getting into too much trouble. And still, after I did my Leaving Cert I went on to join the Redemptorists. I wonder why I did it. The fact that my two brothers had gone this route before me and that following in their footsteps had become the pattern of my life was undoubtedly a big factor. There was also the sense that I needed to do this in order to assure my eternal salvation.

Did I have a vocation? I have no idea how to answer this question, because I would have grave doubts now about this notion of God calling people, especially to this particular ministry of priesthood. I do know that at the age of seventeen years and seven months, one day in August 1964, I dressed up in a black suit, with a flannelette shirt to which was attached a white collar, a black tie and, most incongruous of all, a black hat. I had never worn a hat in my life up to this point. As we didn't have a car at this stage a neighbour brought me the short journey to the local Redemptorist monastery. This man had two sons, who were my companions on the local hurling team all through my teenage years. We had shared many a good day on the field of play. They came to see me off at the crossroads and it was at this point that the incongruity of my attire, especially the hat, really came home to me. I can still remember the embarrassment!

Then I locked myself away in a Redemptorist novitiate for the next thirteen months. Looking back now I can see that this was a big mistake. I was much too young and had far too much to learn about life. As I had always been very active in sport, a largely sedentary year meant that I put on about twenty-five pounds, which was a very unhealthy thing. At the end of this period, I and eleven classmates lined up one day in the small church attached to the monastery and, in the context of a religious ceremony, took vows of poverty, chastity and obedience.

I find it impossible to think back clearly to that time in my life, to discern my level of understanding of what I was doing and to establish what my real motives might possibly have been. It is hard to imagine that I had anything like the maturity needed to make such a decision, even if the vows I took that day were only temporary. I had lived a very sheltered life, both at home and in my years at school. I had never gone out with a girl. By today's standards I was emotionally and sexually retarded. I remember discussing with one of my fellow novices our biggest sacrifice in entering religious life. I was adamant that not being able to take part in sport was what I missed most. He said that he found it hardest to give up his girlfriend. I remember thinking this was very strange.

How could a girlfriend be compared to the excitement of running on to the field with a football or a hurley in my hands?

The novitiate year, even though it was designed as a preparation for the act of public profession, was no help at all, as it was geared totally towards the goal of making our profession and filtered out of our lives any ideas or activities that might introduce thoughts of other ways of living. Instead of being an open year of exploring alternative ways of life it was narrowly and exclusively focused. It was an intense period of brainwashing. I wonder how conscious I was of the notion of obedience that was prevalent in the Redemptorists at that time. It was, at least at the official level, a blind obedience that the will of the superior was the will of God. We were told that the sound of the bell ringing for the various community activities of the day was the voice of God. There was one clear image of God projected in all of this, a God who was summed up in the rules and constitutions of the congregation.

I know now from the stories of my older colleagues that in those times there were superiors who seriously abused their positions of authority, something that is not surprising. To put a human being in a position of power over a community of men when his decisions and orders were seen as those of the Almighty was too much temptation for anyone who was not deeply detached from ego or prejudice. One would need to be very advanced in the spiritual life to avoid abusing such power. Many of the men who found themselves in such positions were clearly not of this calibre and it was wrong to give them such power and more wrong still to have people subject to them. There are many old religious around the country who carry within them the scars of the treatment they received in their young days from bully boy or girl superiors.

Certainly in our novitiate, even though our novice master was a kindly man, we were presented with the traditional idea of obedience. Singularity, or individuality, was discouraged. In submitting our will to that of our superior we were to become part of the group, not standing out or thinking for ourselves. Conformity was the order of the day.

How deeply any of this entered my consciousness, or how seriously I thought about the implications of it before the day of first profession I am not sure. In truth, I suspect that I thought very little about it because the ability to think for myself had been knocked out of me by this stage.

My time in the seminary coincided with the end of the Second Vatican Council. When I began there was a large number of students and by the time I was ordained that number had declined by two thirds at least. They were exciting years. I spent the first three in the university in Galway, studying for an Arts degree. They were the years of student revolt around the world and even as far away from Paris as the west of Ireland there were definite stirrings. The debates in the Literary and Debating Society, as it was called, were boisterous affairs, where all ideas were admitted and sharp ripostes were the order of the day. I remember, maybe with nostalgia, the extraordinary level of energy these debates generated. A meeting in the old Latin Hall on the topic of Vatican II was so crowded that some of the seating collapsed, resulting in a certain degree of panic. I recently attended a student debate in the same college, although in a new building, on the topic of the future of the Church. The old energy had diminished and the crowd had dwindled. We are now in a very different Ireland.

In my student days I never had the courage to stand up and make a contribution at one of these debates but I attended them avidly and loved the cut and thrust of ideas. Even in the seminary itself new ideas were rampant. When I arrived from the novitiate the first two books that were put on the table in my room by the senior student whose responsibility it was to help me settle in were Tolstoy's *War and Peace* and *The Catcher in the Rye*, by J. D. Salinger, that bible of young revolution in the 1960s. ('Sleep on, you morons,' said Holden Caulfield.) Not only were we all reading these types of books, we were discussing them among ourselves. We were listening to the music of the Beatles and Simon and Garfunkel and reading the modern theologians who were prolific in their writing after the Vatican Council. We rediscovered the writings of John Henry Newman on conscience, and loved some of his more quotable quotes. In relation to the bishops and theologians Newman had this to say on conscience:

'I should look to see what theologians could do for me, what the bishops and clergy around me, what my confessor; what friends whom I have revered: and if, after all, I could not take their view of the matter, then I must rule myself by my own judgement and my own conscience.'

And, most attractive of all, his comment in an after-dinner toast:

'Certainly, if I am obliged to bring religion into after-dinner toasts (which indeed does not seem quite the thing), I shall drink, – to the pope, if you please, – still, to conscience first, and to the pope afterwards.'

The Vatican Council documents also emphasised the role of conscience as the final arbiter between a person and God. Soon enough the brainwashing and traditional spirituality of my novitiate year were washed away. Between the atmosphere in the seminary and the free-thinking flow of opinions in the college, a notion like blind obedience didn't have much chance of surviving. Of course many battles were fought out with the authorities during those seminary years, as the old ways of thinking began to give way to the new. Inevitably some of those in charge tried to exercise authority in the dogmatic ways of the past. All the traditional notions of what made a good religious were being challenged and no one was sure any longer the type of formation programme that was needed for the future. If blind obedience to the superior was no longer tenable, what did the vow of obedience mean? The notion of conscience as the final arbiter was not compatible with the idea of such blind obedience.

Gradually, over the years, we began to look on obedience in a very different light. It became more a matter of the consensus of the community than the will of the superior. Religious life changed dramatically and became, over the years of my career, quite good at developing systems where consensus could be achieved. It had a big element of democracy about it, as superiors were elected and served for a specific period of time, but it attempted to move beyond democracy as it is normally exercised in society, by trying as much as possible to make decisions based on consensus rather than on a majority vote, even though on some occasions such a vote might be the only way of reaching a decision. This is not to say that utopia has been achieved, because there is always the danger that consensus becomes the lowest common denominator and the person who swims against the tide is dismissed as a crank.

Be that as it may, when I arrived at my final profession, about eight years after I had made my first one, I had a very different sense of what was involved in the vow of obedience. As life went on, being part of community, serving on councils and acting as superior of a community, I developed and changed my understanding so that I now see obedience as part of a bigger picture that involves at some deep level 'doing the right thing'. When Michael Brehl presented me with a formal precept of obedience, I was taken aback, hardly realising that such a process still existed in religious life. When the document he had promised arrived I read it with amazement:

'Dear Father Tony
'In our telephone conversation yesterday I communicated to you the decision of the Congregation for the Doctrine of the Faith that your response to its request for a statement of your complete adherence to the doctrine of the Catholic Faith was incomplete and therefore unacceptable. I shared with you the instructions of the Congregation that you continue your period of prayer and study

until such time as you had arrived at a satisfactory statement, as well as the conditions under which you are to spend this period.

'I also let you know that the Congregation had regretfully found it unacceptable for you to participate in or attend the Annual General Meeting of the ACP on November 10, 2012 and requested me to instruct you, under religious obedience, to cancel your attendance at this meeting. Since you have not been able to give me an assurance that you would follow this instruction, I am therefore obliged to issue you a formal precept of obedience obliging you to carry it out. You are hereby formally asked to cancel your planned attendance at this meeting and not to have any part in its deliberations.

'I regret that it has become necessary to formally invoke the obedience which you professed in our congregation and I fervently hope and pray that you will have the grace to obey my precept 'willingly and promptly' as Number 73 of our constitutions urges you to do.

'Fr Tony, I am very aware that you are in a very difficult situation and I am anxious to offer to help in every way that I can.

'May the intercession of Mary, our Mother of Perpetual Succour and the prayers of our Holy Father Alphonsus obtain for you the strength to renew your fidelity to Jesus, our Most Holy Redeemer, at this painful moment in your life.

'With fraternal good wishes'

In fairness to Michael Brehl, unlike the CDF people, he was willing to sign his name to this letter and it was written on proper headed notepaper. I suppose there was nothing in it that was too surprising, as the phone call that preceded it had gone over the same ground. It was probably for this reason that I was most irritated by the last sentence, where he put in the prayer. He had no doubt that 'fidelity to Jesus' meant that I should do what I was told. I believed the opposite. I was also struck by the frequency with which people in the Church use the concept of prayer to impose their will on others and stifle further discussion. Among the many letters of support I got from around the world was one from a Baptist pastor in Australia. She summed this idea up beautifully in one paragraph of her letter:

'I am writing to encourage you as daily you have to face the doubts and fears that leave you wondering over and over again whether perhaps "they" are correct and you are in reality somewhat deluded and following your own agenda, rather than listening to the true and rational word of God which they claim to know and interpret unerringly. Always "'they" assure you that they have your best interests at heart and they are hoping and, indeed, praying that you will soon come to your senses and return to the fold where they will welcome you and rejoice over your change of heart – and incidentally taking this course of action will have the added benefit of making life easier for yourself!'

I knew immediately that I could not obey the precept. I regarded it as unfair and unjust and felt that it was an abuse of the concept of obedience as I understood it. After nearly a year of dealing with Michael Brehl, this was the point at which we arrived at a parting of the ways. I know it would have been extremely difficult for him to stand up to the CDF, given the imbalance of power that was obvious in his relations with that body. However, I think he missed an excellent opportunity for taking a stand. I believed that the record of my life in the Redemptorists did not in any way justify issuing me with a formal precept of obedience, especially one that concerned nothing more than attending a meeting. I have since checked with many of my fellow Redemptorists and nobody could remember anyone receiving such a document. The precept cast me in the role of a troublesome religious and, without being too judgemental, I considered that there were colleagues who might be considered much more troublesome.

In addition to my standing in the Redemptorists there was a

more serious issue at stake, the independence of the Association of Catholic Priests. We cherished the fact that we were an independent body, although we were well aware that we were an anomaly in the Church and that the authorities were not too sure how to deal with us. If I stayed away from the meeting, under orders from the CDF and the Redemptorist superior, I would be conceding that the Church authorities had the right to decide who could and could not belong to the ACP or attend its meetings. If this happened we might as well close down because we would be in exactly the same position as the priests' organisation that was in existence before us, which had collapsed through lack of interest. So I composed a reply to Fr Brehl:

'Dear Michael
'I received your letter today.

'I have been a member of the congregation for forty-seven years. While I make no claim to have been a perfect religious, I have spent those years working to spread the message of Jesus Christ in accordance with the spirit and charism of the Redemptorist congregation. I have been involved with the Association of Catholic Priests for over two years. No Redemptorist superior, at any level, has expressed any reservation to me, either verbally or in writing, about my activities in this association.

'It is my understanding that such a precept as I have now received should come only at the end of a process where I had been acquainted, in writing, with the matters of concern that my congregation has in relation to my involvement with the ACP.

'I also wish to draw your attention to the fact that your formal precept that I do not attend the meeting on 10 November is in direct contradiction of the rights that I have as an Irish citizen under the constitution of the Irish Republic. These constitutional rights are fundamental and inalienable and are for the protection of all Irish citizens, be they priests or lay people. Any exercise of authority by an organ within the Irish State, be that organ religious or other, must be cognisant of and must not offend these rights. As one adviser who has a qualification in both civil and canon law has stated: "To prohibit membership of or attendance at a perfectly legitimate body would in my view be as canonically unsound as it would be constitutionally unsound, not to mention being an infringement of your rights set out in various international and European human rights treaties to which the Holy See is a signatory."

'I regret that the situation has come to this. I appreciate that you too are in a very difficult position and I am aware that it is highly unlikely that you would have issued this precept if the Congregation for the Doctrine of the Faith had not instructed you to do so. I also point out that my statement of 29 September was not, in my view, 'incomplete'. I responded to each point that had been presented to me in an unsigned document. I can only conclude that my statement did not meet the requirements of the CDF because it was a true statement of my belief rather than the kind of statement which the CDF wanted. I regret that I cannot tailor my conscience to other people's needs and expectations.

'I consider that it is only right to inform you that if you proceed with this course of action I will defend myself in every way that is available to me.'

The memory of walking in the door of the hotel where the association was holding its AGM is still clearly etched in my mind. It was an emotional moment. I knew that I was in a real sense crossing the Rubicon and that finding a way back would be difficult, to say the least, yet I didn't have any doubt that I was doing the right thing. The people attending the meeting were not aware of the significance of my being there and I was glad to keep it from them. It was an important step in the formation of a new association for lay Catholics and I did not want anything to distract attention from this. I met some of my own Redemptorist colleagues during the meeting and updated them on what was happening. I judged that my presence there would be reported to Rome before the meeting had ended and, to add fuel to the fire, I agreed to do a short piece for the main evening news on RTÉ TV about the theme of the conference. Two days later I received the following email from Michael Brehl:

'Dear Father Tony
'In my letter of October 29th, following instructions received from the Congregation for the Doctrine of the Faith, I instructed you in a formal manner not to participate at the AGM of the ACP on November 10th. When you replied by email on November 2nd and indicated that you could not give me an assurance that you would not participate at the meeting, I formally repeated the prohibition. I am now reliably informed that you chose to ignore my instructions and that you participated in the two-day meeting.

'I regret very much that it became necessary for me to give you those formal instructions, but it is a matter of much greater sorrow to me that you chose to ignore these explicit directions. I now wish to remind you that as a Redemptorist religious priest you have failed in a serious way against the obedience you have professed in the congregation and thereby seriously weakened your position within the congregation. If this kind of disobedience to the lawfully and formally expressed wishes of superiors continues there could be very serious consequences to follow. Fr Tony, once again, I appeal to you as a Redemptorist confrère and as a priest to follow the instructions you have received.

'In view of your involvement with the Association from its be-ginning, I understood that my instruction placed you in a position of having to make quite a painful choice but I hoped and prayed that you would follow faithfully your vowed commitment in the congregation and follow my instructions. You chose not to do so and I cannot ignore your errant behaviour. Nevertheless, I am conscious that you accepted not to make public your position and thereby avoided any negative public reaction to this decision taken at the behest of the Congregation for the Doctrine of the Faith.

'I hope that this choice on your part might be a signal that you are ready to take up again the process of finding an acceptable statement of your adherence to Catholic Church teaching. I look forward to a positive reaction on your part to my appeal once again to find an acceptable way to do so.

'In Christ the Redeemer'

I got the message clearly. I had made it clear to Michael Brehl a number of times that I could not give the CDF the statement they were looking for and that the statement I had given was my final position spelt out as clearly as I could. I can understand why Michael Brehl did not want to hear this as my actions put him in a very awkward position vis-à-vis the Vatican authorities. I did resent the fact that, in the last paragraph, he equated the demand of the CDF with 'Catholic Church teaching'. I certainly disagreed with him on this score. It was Vatican teaching but I believed it did not have the necessary acceptance by the faithful to make it Church teaching.

Brehl's letter was a clear acknowledgement that he would never have considered imposing a formal precept of obedience on me if the CDF had not put the gun to his head; there was a perception among my confrères in the Redemptorists that if he had not 'cooperated' with the Vatican his position as head of the congregation would be in jeopardy. But an interesting precedent existed, which concerned a situation very similar to mine. This involved the well-known American Benedictine sister, Joan Chittister. In 2001, she was invited to speak at a conference on women's ordination in Dublin. The Vatican issued a similar 'request' to her superior, that she put Chittister under formal precept of obedience not to address the gathering. Prioress Christine Vladimiroff refused, citing 'a fundamental difference [between] the understanding of obedience in the monastic tradition' and that used by the Vatican. She said she did not see Chittister's participation in the conference as 'a source of scandal to the faithful' as the Vatican alleged. Rather, she continued, the faithful are 'scandalised when honest attempts to discuss questions of import to the Church are forbidden'. How right she was, as evidenced by the scandal that ensued when the Church did not honestly and openly discuss the problem of clerical child sexual abuse.

I did not respond to Michael Brehl's email myself as I could see no point in doing so. I knew what he wanted and that it would be pointless for me to engage with him again. The CDF was still treating me largely as a non-person and as long as it was not willing to engage directly with me there was no chance of progress.

After taking appropriate advice I had already decided that I would not go down the route of using canon law to defend myself. The cards would be stacked against me if I did. I would be playing the game on the Vatican pitch, under its rules, with the CDF as the referee. Instead I consulted the legal team that was working for the ACP. The lawyers were amazed at CDF procedures, which they regarded as being completely contrary to the processes that were normal in civil law. They couldn't understand why I didn't have possession of all the relevant documents. There was an exchange of letters between the solicitor acting for me and one acting for Fr Brehl, who asserted that this was a matter between a religious and his superior and that it did not come under the jurisdiction of civil law.

17

An End to Silence

At this stage almost a year had passed since I had the first intimations of difficulties with the CDF. In all this time I had not spoken publicly about them, although aspects of the story had gone public. I had been out of ministry, back for a while, then out again. Apart from my colleagues in the Redemptorists and those close to me, most people weren't really aware of my situation. This was difficult for me. I was finding myself in embarrassing situations when people asked me to celebrate Mass, officiate at a baptism or preach a mission in their parish and I had to explain that I wasn't allowed to do so. I was having a lot of unreal conversations. People weren't quite sure what to say to me, nor did I know what to say to them, whether I should tell them about my current situation or not. I was in a kind of limbo, my life was on hold and I felt a real need to take some control over it.

By the end of the year I had also come to the conclusion that, unless something extraordinary happened, there was no way I was ever going to be allowed to minister as a priest again. So I judged that there was nothing worse that the Church authorities could do to me. They could excommunicate me but I regarded this as a medieval concept that had no meaning in the modern world. I knew that no document from Rome would prevent me from being part of the Church and partaking in the sacraments. The CDF could order the Redemptorists to dismiss me from the congregation, as they had done to others, most recently Roy Bourgeois of the Maryknoll congregation in the US. But if I wasn't going to be able to minister I had to ask myself why I would want to remain in a Redemptorist community for the rest of my life. For me the work that I did as a priest was what attracted me to the congregation. I loved preaching the message and engaging with people. The living out of religious life never did appeal very much to me and anyway, with the current state of religious life, our communities are effectively old people's homes.

This came home to me on one occasion in the early months of 2013, when the four more active members of my community were away preaching a novena while I was at home with the older men. It was a particularly interesting week, with a number of very significant events happening in both the religious and political sphere, both in our own country and worldwide. (Pope Benedict resigned and the former Anglo Irish Bank was liquidated, resolving the promissory note issue.) But nobody in the community was capable of conducting a conversation about such matters. The older men were largely oblivious of what was happening in the world outside. It came home to me strongly that week that living in this type of set-up, while not being allowed to work, could be very detrimental to my wellbeing.

When my colleagues came home from the novena late on the final evening I joined them for a drink and a chat in the community room. They had been working on one of our large annual novenas, one that I had helped to set up and had participated in many times. They were tired after nine intense days but elated by the success of the novena. I had often returned from a similar event in a similar state of excitement so, while I could empathise with them as they related their experience, I realised that from now on I was going to be an outsider.

In January 2013 I decided to go public. I knew that my story had a certain significance as it reflected similar occurrences around the Catholic Church. Here in Ireland, we could count at least five priests whose writings had been censored by Rome. I believed that by revealing my experience with Church authority I would add to the pressure for change that was building up around the world. I still had a great attachment to the Church and since I could not do my priestly work, I concluded that the best contribution I could make at this time was to expose the unjust procedures of the Vatican and its serious abuse of power, which I was convinced was causing great damage to the Church.

I was lucky to have had the very generous advice of a media professional, who guided me through the whole process. The first thing I did was to give an interview to the reporter for the *New York Times*, on condition that it would not be published until I gave the signal, which was on the morning of Sunday 20 January, when I held a press conference. This is the text of the press statement I issued:

'Redemptorist Subjected to 'Frightening Procedures Reminiscent of the Inquisition'

'Redemptorist Fr Tony Flannery is threatened with excommunication from the Catholic Church for suggesting that, in the future, women might become priests and calling for this and other matters to be open for discussion. Fr Flannery (66), who joined the Redemptorists in 1964 at seventeen and was ordained ten years later, has been told that if he is to remain in the Church and in his congregation, he must also guarantee not to attend meetings of the Association of Catholic Priests (ACP) until he has publicly agreed to the conditions laid down.

'Fr Flannery was forbidden to minister as a priest for most of the past year and this will continue until he meets the requirements of the Congregation for the Doctrine of the Faith.

'"I have been ordered not to engage with the media or publish any books or articles," he told a press briefing in Dublin today. "I have also been ordered not to have any involvement, public or private, with the ACP. I was put under a formal precept of obedience not to attend the AGM of the ACP last November by

Michael Brehl, Superior General of the Redemptorists. But he made it clear he'd been instructed by the CDF to issue it.'

'Fr Flannery will be allowed back into ministry only if he writes, signs and publishes an article (pre-approved by the CDF) accepting the Catholic Church can never ordain women to the priesthood and accepting all Church stances on contraception, homosexuality, and the refusal of the sacraments to people in second relationships.

'"I could not possibly put my name to such an article without impugning my own integrity and conscience," he said today. "The Congregation for the Doctrine of the Faith is orchestrating all this while refusing to communicate with me. I have had no direct communication with them. I have never been given an opportunity to meet my accusers, or to understand why this action is being taken against me, when I've raised the same issues, consistently, for decades."

'The documentation Fr Flannery received, apparently from the CDF, took the form of a typed A4 page (not a letterhead) which was unsigned.

'"The only reason that I can be sure that this came from the CDF is that Michael Brehl, the head of the Redemptorists, told me it did," he said. "All requests for direct communication with the CDF have been ignored."

'Fr Flannery described as "frightening, disproportionate and reminiscent of the Inquisition" the actions against him.

'"I have served the Church, the Redemptorists and the people of God for two thirds of my life," he pointed out. "Throughout that time, I have in good conscience raised issues I believed important for the future of the Church in books and essays largely read by practising Catholics, rather than raising them in mainstream media. I'm hardly a major and subversive figure within the Church deserving excommunication and expulsion from the religious community within which I have lived since my teens."

'The choice facing him, he stated at a press briefing today,

Sunday 20 January, was deciding between Rome and his conscience.

"'I must also question if the threats are a means, not just of terrifying me into submission, but of sending a message to any other priest expressing views at variance with those of the Roman Curia," he added. "Submitting to these threats would be a betrayal of my ministry, my fellow priests and the Catholic people who want change."

'Fr Flannery said that because he believes he is being subjected to unfair treatment, he has taken legal advice under canon and civil law to help him defend his rights as a member of the Church and as an Irish citizen.'

Now that the news was out I had an extremely busy few weeks, with a great many media outlets looking for the story. During these weeks I came to appreciate very much the value of professional guidance because when one is dealing with the media, not everything will be presented in the way one might wish. But generally I was happy that I had got the message out with a reasonable degree of accuracy, especially in the international media. Any significant negative criticism that was levelled at me came from the Catholic papers in Ireland, something that didn't surprise me, as these newspapers have not been supporters of the ACP since they first got word that we planned to launch an association.

I was aware that my action in going public would cause difficulty for the Redemptorists and I had promised the Irish superior that I would give him adequate notice of it. I told him about a week in advance and he met the provincial council, the governing body of the Redemptorists in Ireland, a few times, so that they would be ready to respond when the time came. On the Sunday evening after my press conference, they issued a statement which was released to the media and put up on the Irish Redemptorist website. It was very supportive of me and raised questions about the processes of the CDF:

Sunday 20 January 2013

'The Irish Redemptorist community is deeply saddened by the breakdown in communication between Fr Tony Flannery CSsR and the Congregation for the Doctrine of the Faith (CDF).

'Fr Tony Flannery is highly regarded and respected by many in Ireland, both within and outside of the Redemptorist Congregation. He has been an effective parish missioner all over the country since the mid 1970s and from this context has raised matters which he believes need greater dialogue, debate and consideration. Within the Dublin province of the Redemptorists there exists a very lively spirit of debate and dialogue; we are and over many years have been, committed to mature discourse. Although not all Redemptorists would accept Fr Flannery's views on all matters, we do understand and support his efforts to listen carefully to and at times to articulate the views of people he encounters in the course of his ministry.

'As Irish Redemptorists we appreciate the difficulties this situation has created for others, especially for our superior general in Rome, Fr Michael Brehl. He has made every possible effort to resolve the matters which have emerged between the CDF and Fr Flannery.

'Our Redemptorist constitutions require us to be obedient to God's call to us as religious in the Church. Following our founder, St Alphonsus, for whom thinking with the Church was an important criterion of missionary service, a further key element of our Church mandate is to listen and stay close to God's people; to engage in missionary dialogue with the world while endeavouring to understand people's anxious questionings; to try to discover in these how God is truly being revealed.

'It is of immense regret that some structures or processes of dialogue have not yet been found in the Church which have a greater capacity to engage with challenging voices from among God's people, while respecting the key responsibility and central role of the Congregation for the Doctrine of the Faith.

'We sincerely hope and pray that even at this late stage, some agreed resolution can be found to this matter.'

I was acutely aware that, in writing this statement, the men of the governing council had to take a lot into consideration. They had to be conscious how the statement would be read in the Vatican, by the general government of the congregation in Rome, by Redemptorist colleagues in Ireland and by the Catholic public. I thought they did really well and my initial reaction was that this statement might cause more concern in the Vatican than anything I was doing. I knew that the council was conscious of the fact that when my story first broke the previous April a number of individual Redemptorists went public in support of me. They now wanted to avoid a situation in which Redemptorists would voice their individual opinions in public, creating the impression that the Irish Redemptorists was a province in revolt. I learned later that the provincial had warned each of the likely suspects that if even one of them spoke out of turn, he would be forced to resign. I believe this put enormous moral pressure on them to stay silent.

Two days later things changed: the statement of the Irish province was removed from our website, to be replaced by a very different statement from Michael Brehl, one that could not be viewed as supportive of me:

Statement by Most Rev Fr Michael Brehl CSsR, Superior General of the Redemptorists

'As Superior General of the Congregation of the Most Holy Redeemer, I deeply regret the recent actions undertaken by Father Tony Flannery, CSsR

'In January, 2012, the Congregation for the Doctrine of the Faith raised concerns about some of the writings of Fr Flannery which were ambiguous regarding fundamental areas of Catholic doctrine, including the priesthood, the nature of the Church, and the Eucharist. He was instructed to undertake a period of prayer and theological reflection to clarify his positions on these matters. During this sabbatical period, he was instructed not to grant interviews or make public statements, and to withdraw from active involvement in the leadership of the ACP, especially since the priesthood was one of the matters on which he was asked to clarify his position. He was also instructed to withdraw from active priestly ministry during this period of prayer and reflection.

'Once again, I earnestly invite my confrère Fr Flannery to renew the efforts to find an agreed solution to the concerns raised by the Congregation for the Doctrine of the Faith.

'Finally, I invite my Redemptorist confrères of the Irish province to join with me in praying and working together in the spirit of St Alphonsus to maintain and strengthen our communion with the universal Church.'

I was very disappointed by this statement. I didn't think that it gave a fair representation of the process that I had engaged in for almost a year with Brehl and the CDF. It totally ignored the fact that I had given a statement which, he said, had clarified the matters concerning priesthood. Brehl's email to me in June, after his meeting with Cardinal Levada, when he delivered my first statement, said that I had effectively put the accusation of heresy to bed and that we could move on from there. This new statement chose to ignore this. He also failed to recognise that the breaking point had come when the CDF had added issues in September about which they had difficulties – issues that were not part of their original complaints in February. Brehl was now calling on me to renew my efforts to find an agreed solution, although he knew perfectly well that there was only one possible solution open to me: to give the CDF the statement they looked for. He must have known that the CDF, having rejected my most recent statement, was not going to back down and I had made it clear to him that my statement of late September was my final one.

I regarded his words about an 'agreed solution' as a fudge and the most charitable interpretation I can put on this statement is that it was written for and under orders from the Vatican. The only other conclusion I can draw is that he is more of a victim in this situation than I am: that while he is ostensibly in a position of authority over a worldwide congregation, when it comes to the crunch, he doesn't have any power at all. He has to do exactly what he is told, even if he does not believe in it. When I look back I realise that I had earlier evidence of this when he put my formal precept of obedience in writing. From what I know of him, I don't see how he could have been happy writing that letter.

As time went on I became aware that these two actions of the superior general caused a great deal of anger and disappointment among some of my colleagues in the congregation. The whole experience of what happened to the Irish Redemptorists in the weeks after my press conference was an example of how authority in the Church works and why it is so dysfunctional. Michael Brehl's statement had became the official Redemptorist response, even though it was at odds with the real position of the Irish province. Meanwhile individual Redemptorists who may have wished to make their voices heard were effectively silenced. It seemed as if the institution was closing ranks and the leadership imposing its authority by fair means or foul. The last sentence of Michael Brehl's statement epitomised this. Criticism of the Church would not be tolerated, even if many of the members at least partially subscribed to it. As a Catholic religious body, apparently our duty was to maintain and strengthen our communion with the universal Church.

I began to realise that my actions had effectively put me out of the system, that no matter how supportive my colleagues were at a personal level and how much they agreed with a great many of my views, I was outside and they were inside. In some quarters the word going around was that Michael Brehl was doing the best he could, that he had to think of the good of the whole congregation and not do anything that would allow the Vatican to move him aside and replace him with their own candidate.

As the weeks went on a small number of my fellow Redemptorists, who would have supported me at first, began to lose patience. As one man put it: 'It is time for Tony Flannery to shut up now, to go and sign that document and get on with his ministry.' But many others remained steadfast in their support and some were possibly even more disillusioned by what had happened than I was myself. As another colleague put it: 'When I took my vows I thought I was making them to the congregation; I now wonder was it to the CDF.'

18

Corruption in the Vatican

During the whole of that frustrating year of trying to deal with the Vatican without having any direct contact with them, I had the underlying belief that the curial system, the 'civil service' of the Catholic Church that made up the Vatican organisation, was dysfunctional or, to use the modern phrase, not fit for purpose. We in the ACP had a suspicion that there might be some more serious and sinister dysfunction. The Vatileaks scandal and the various sagas relating to the Vatican Bank raised such questions in our minds. Over the past thirty years or so the Vatican had taken more and more power and control to itself, as I had experienced over the previous year. The American Jesuit theologian, Thomas Reese wrote in the *National Catholic Reporter:*

'The papacy is operating like the absolute monarchies of the 17th century where the monarch held the legislative, executive and judicial powers. Modern governments recognise the need for a separation of powers. Agencies like the Congregation for the Doctrine of the Faith should not make the rules, and then act as police, prosecutor, judge, jury and executor in dealing with theologians. This is not due process in the modern sense.'

Any organisation that has such power and puts such store on secrecy will almost inevitably succumb to corruption in time but when we in the ACP dared to air these views in public, even tentatively, we were heavily criticised.

But then Pope Benedict XVI announced his retirement in February 2013 and everything changed. During the weeks between this announcement and the election of his successor, Pope Francis, open discussion broke out at all levels in the Church. Suddenly all our best lines, the statements that had got us into trouble, were being stolen by senior officials in the Church, even by cardinals. It quickly became an accepted fact that the Vatican was dysfunctional and in urgent need of reform. Words as strong as 'corrupt' and 'dishonest' were being thrown around. It was in this context that I listened to a radio interview given by Archbishop Diarmaid Martin a week or so after Pope Francis had been elected. When asked whether the Vatileaks scandal had damaged the Church, he assented: 'Any system that uses information to damage somebody else, then something rotten has got into an organisation like that.'

Using the word 'rotten' about the Vatican was strong stuff. He continued: 'I worked in the Vatican for many years. I met some great people; I met some very nasty people; I met some very ambitious people, in the bad sense of that word. When you see people who not only are ambitious for themselves but who are prepared to walk on others as part of that, that is not the Church.' And when asked why it was that there had not been reform before now, he replied: 'Organisations and structures and institutions have a habit of keeping going and of defending themselves.'

This confirmed for me something I had often suspected. For many years I had observed priests who went from dioceses and religious orders to work in the Vatican. Some of them were good and capable but there were others who seemed to fit into the category Dr Martin mentioned: men who were intensely ambitious for advancement within the Church. For somebody like this a diocese or a religious congregation does not hold out much promise of advancement. In religious congregations a person might reach a position of prominence but it would be for only a set period of time; then he would return to the ranks. In a diocese, unless one is lucky (or unlucky) enough to be chosen as a bishop, there is little promotion to strive for. The days when titles like 'monsignor', 'canon' or 'dean' meant much have long gone. For an ambitious cleric the Vatican was the place to go. Clearly the combination of power without accountability, strict secrecy and men who, according to Archbishop Martin, were so ambitious that they were willing to walk on others in order to achieve their goals, makes for a very dangerous mixture.

The other kind of priest I observed ending up in the Vatican was one who did not fit into the diocesan system or who could not relate to the people at parish level, perhaps due to extreme eccentricity or an outdated theological fundamentalism. In either case this type of person is unsuited for a position of authority. Another disturbing feature is the way some US cardinals who had been less than distinguished in running their own dioceses were given positions of significance in the Curia.

There are major questions surrounding another scandal that continues to reveal new and astonishing features: the story of Marcial Maciel Degollado. This priest founded a large and very traditional religious order known as the Legionaries of Christ, and also a lay institute, Regnum Christi. He was a great friend of Pope John Paul II and of Cardinal Soldano, one of the most powerful people in the Vatican. He died in 2008 and it is now clear that not only did he have children by two different women but, much more disturbing, he had abused some of his seminarians and even his own children. He was also possibly the greatest fundraiser the Church has ever known. The religious order he founded is immensely wealthy but of much greater concern is the report that he poured enormous amounts of money into the Vatican, including, reputedly, funding most of Pope John Paul's foreign trips.

Many questions need to be answered regarding this man and his relationship with the Vatican establishment. How could he continue to be welcomed and honoured by the Pope and the Curia long after it became clear that there were such serious concern about him? Facing up to these questions will have to be part of the programme of the new Pope if he really wishes to make a fresh start.

19

An Uncertain Future

As I write this, the final chapter of my account of my dealings with the Vatican, it is six months since the press conference in which I first went public. I remain out of ministry, with no real prospects of ever being allowed back. In those six months I have had no communication of any nature from the Vatican and nothing personal from my own superior general. He has been in Ireland, I attended a meeting at which he was present and we had a pleasant, sociable exchange. There was a meeting between him and a large group of Redemptorists, which was meant to be an open forum to deal with any issues that people wanted to bring up. As it transpired, the whole two hours was taken up discussing my situation. Since it was a private meeting it would not be right for me to reveal any details of it but I was very encouraged by the support I got at the meeting.

In recent times I have had a number of meetings with the Irish superior of the Redemptorists. He is trying hard to find a way out of this situation and I appreciate his efforts, even though I don't have much hope of success. People who know the Vatican have told me that there are indications that not everyone in the CDF is singing from the same hymn sheet, that there are some who wish that this had been handled differently. It has also been suggested to me that I have caused the Vatican more embarrassment than they thought I was capable of. In this context I have been asked if I would consider giving a further statement, maybe conceding something of my previous stance, in order to test this theory and see if there is a possibility that the CDF would respond with some positive overtures. I would much prefer to have more definite signals from the CDF to encourage me to enter into a further round of 'negotiations' with the Vatican. If I got some direct communication from them, rather than in the usual roundabout fashion, I would certainly be happy to respond positively. It seems such a small thing to ask, such a basic act of human decency, that they would correspond directly with me. But I know from my experience that this will not happen.

The major events that have occurred in the Church since my press conference have been the resignation of Pope Benedict and, after a very interesting interregnum, the election of Francis as pope. Now, wherever I go, people ask me: 'Have you heard anything from the Vatican? Will Francis make a difference to your situation?' There is a perception that Francis is really changing things and that maybe cases like mine will be handled differently in the future.

Francis does seem to be changing some things. He is certainly very different from the popes who have gone before him. Up to this point his changes are more style than substance – not that I would in any way downplay the importance of a change in style, as, when it comes to the papacy, perception may be nearly as important as reality. It will take a few months before we can say with any certainty whether he will seriously take on the difficult task of reforming the Curia, which, to my surprise, became a big feature of the cardinals' discussions before the conclave began. I tell people that I do not expect any immediate changes that will influence my situation, although I do agree with those who say there will probably be a change in the way this type of problem is dealt with in the future. There may well be less dogmatic arrogance and I would hope that there will be less trampling on the basic human rights of individuals. Some procedures may well be worked out to deal with such issues at local church level, at least at the initial stages. But that is for the future. What has been decided will not change. The Vatican does not do climb-downs or u-turns.

Whatever happens from here on in my dealings with the

Vatican, I have decided that there are two things on which I will not compromise. I will not make any secret deal with the Vatican. If there is any change in our relationship it will be out in the open. This is of great importance to me. Secrecy has been the most oppressive aspect of this whole saga and indeed of the way the Vatican operates, so I will not become involved with anything secretive again.

Secondly, I will not accept a return to ministry at the price of silence, any arrangement that involves a series of sanctions or imposes conditions about what I can speak or write about. Freedom of speech is central to human dignity.

People regularly ask me how I am. The answer is complex and I do not usually burden or bore my questioner by going into details about it. At this stage it is more than a year since I was forbidden to minister as a priest. This has been difficult: I miss being able to celebrate the Eucharist and the other sacraments and I miss being able to preach. I know I can say Mass privately but I seldom do so, except when I am with one or two friends. Celebrating Mass on my own has never been a meaningful exercise for me because I believe that the Mass is essentially a community experience. So I mostly attend Mass with the people.

The experience of living in my religious community and mixing with other Redemptorists has changed greatly for me. Recently I was visiting one of our other communities and I met a colleague with whom I had worked on missions and novenas down through the years. He talked to me about the work he was doing, the parishes where he had been conducting missions over the past months and how successful they had been. As he spoke I found myself increasingly detached from what he was saying. It no longer interested me in the way that it would have done in the past. It was not a part of my life any longer. In the church attached to my own community there is an annual novena, which has taken place for nine days in June every year since the 1970s. I have often worked on it and I know the people very well. I always loved those days: they had a special atmosphere of friendliness and warmth, with the added dimension of catching up with news of people's lives and having lots of fun and laughter. But this year I stayed only for the first day. I was no longer comfortable at this event and I felt that my presence would put a damper on the sense of celebration which is so much a part of these big novenas. At times like this the realisation of what I have lost comes home to me.

Having been out of ministry and in conflict with Church authorities for an extended period has had a significant impact on my perspective on the Church but more fundamentally on my faith and my life. I have come to know a great deal about how the Church operates, particularly its management structures and methods of decision-making, that I would probably be better off not knowing. Sadly, I have found it to be true that the closer you get to the Vatican system, with all its power struggles and careerism, the more disillusioned you can become. I know that faith in Jesus Christ is more important than any of this but while I can accept this totally at an intellectual level, it is much more difficult to deal with my emotional responses to it. The Church introduced me to Christ and for my whole life my faith has been lived out within the Church, most of it in religious life. So I suppose I am now experiencing something of a crisis of faith.

Even while attending Mass, as I do regularly, I sit there listening to the priest struggle with the new translation of the missal, especially with the opening prayers and prefaces, and I know that whoever was behind this new translation was not motivated by the desire to make the Eucharist more meaningful for the people, but by a rigid ideological stance that had little or nothing to do with the teachings of the Gospel. I wonder at times if some of the people in high positions within the Church are more motivated by personal ambition and the pursuit of power than by a commitment to the message of Jesus. Pope Francis's statement that there is a 'stream of corruption' within the Curia seemed to confirm what I suspected. As a preacher for so many years I was focused on the basic Christian message and tended to keep well away from the type of questions that are now assuming a larger dimension in my consciousness. I suppose this is what happens when one finds oneself standing outside the system, rather than being at the heart of it. I don't know where all this will lead me: I am reasonably at ease with it and willing to let it take its course in my life, if I am given the time to work it out. And if not, then let what will be happen.

In the meantime I have some major decisions to make – or maybe they will be taken out of hands and made by others. I recently spoke to a friend of Roy Bourgeois, the American Maryknoll priest who was dismissed from his congregation and from the priesthood. Maybe this will happen to me. I do not know. Assuming that things do not come to this sorry pass, I will have to decide if I wish to stay in religious life for the time that is remaining to me, without being allowed to carry out any form of ministry. At this point I do not know what effect this would have on me long term, but it may be difficult. Religious life is in a sad state now, anyway, with most of the members of the community in which I live over eighty years of age. The alternative would be to move out on my own and try to make a life for myself but this, quite frankly, is frightening. Would I be able to cope, after living almost my whole life in an institutional setting? Who would look after me in my old age? Would I be very lonely? What about the financial side of it all? Would I have enough to live on? These are the real and hard questions that are occupying my mind at this time.

The Association of Catholic Priests has been an important part of my life for the past three years. Even though I had worked in parishes around the country all my life as a priest, becoming involved with the association enabled me to get to know the real lives of priests much more closely. I have witnessed the stresses and strains of their lives, the loneliness and isolation of some as they grow older and the desperate efforts of others to keep working to the end, because their work is often the only channel that brings them into contact with people. I have dealt with a good many priests who had the experience of a ghost from the past coming to haunt them and turning their lives upside down. I have got a clear view of their faults and failings. I have seen how often even the best of them are inclined to cling on to their power and control rather than cede any real decision-making to the people of the parish. Sometimes I wonder how much faith some of them have, or if they are just doing a job. Even if this were the case I would not judge them for it. All in all I have come to respect and admire them as a body of old men and I would say with certainty that the Church authorities, those in the Vatican and many of the bishops, do not deserve them and have too often treated them badly. I hope that they will get their reward.

I will face into the future with as much energy and life as I can summon up and I will make whatever decisions I need to make as I go along. More than anything else I do not want to waste much more of my time attempting to deal with the Roman authorities in the way I have been trying to do for the past eighteen months. I know for sure this would not be good for me. I have seen other religious being broken down and becoming embittered by their experience. I will try not to let this happen to me. I hope that my faith in a loving and gracious God will survive and take me to a place of peace, whatever the circumstances.

To finish the story, I decided that I would give a further statement to my superiors and ask them to bring it to the Vatican. This is it:

'I have been asked by my superiors to provide a further statement for presentation to the Congregation for the Doctrine of the Faith. I have already submitted two statements. Initially I was led to believe that the first one was deemed 'a very fine statement'. In September I was informed that the Congregation for the Doctrine of the Faith was now requesting that I make a precise, public statement on two further matters, the question of the ordination of women and the moral teaching of the Church. I have been asked to state clearly and publicly that I fully accept that women can never be ordained priests in the Catholic Church and that I accept all the moral teaching of the Church.

'In the early part of 2012, the primary complaint against me related to certain sentences taken from articles written for the Redemptorist magazine, *Reality*. This had mostly to do with the question of priesthood. I sent a statement in response to this, the one I was informed Cardinal Levada described as 'a very fine statement'.

'In an effort to provide further clarification, I wish to outline the context within which these articles were written and the context of the articles from which the sentences were taken. I regard this as being of crucial importance.

'Here in Ireland we have gone through a period of years when horrific revelations of clerical sexual abuse of children became public. This was a very difficult time for all believers and for priests. The revelations coincided with an almost total collapse in vocations to the priesthood, with most seminaries closing. It is important to state that the drop-off in vocations was happening well before the exposure of what is now termed the sexual abuse scandal. All the indications are that in twenty years time there will be very few priests to celebrate the Eucharist for the people. These dramatic developments, so difficult for us all to live through, led inevitably to a wide-ranging and very necessary discussion on priesthood in the Church. It was in this context I was writing.

'I freely admit that some of the sentences that were highlighted by the CDF were not well crafted and were open to various inter-pretations, especially when taken out of context. I hoped that the statement I delivered in June of last year had cleared up this matter.

'I accept that the current position of the Magisterium is that women can never be ordained to the priesthood in the Church but in conscience I do not agree with this position and I gave my reasons more fully in my statement of last September. For me to publicly state that I do accept this would be a lie and a violation of my conscience.

'There are some particular aspects of the Church's sexual teaching to which I cannot give total assent, as I also outlined in my September statement.

'The views I hold on these matters are widely held throughout the Church and both matters have been discussed and debated right around the Church during the whole of my priesthood. Despite the current position of the Magisterium, the debate continues.

'I wish to remain in ministry as a priest. I have tried to remain faithful to the teaching of Christ as outlined in the Scriptures. While I deeply miss presiding at the Eucharist, I accept that in the last analysis I must be ruled by my conscience and in the formation of this I have paid attention to the teaching Magisterium of the Church. I regret that in regard to the two further issues that were raised in September 2012, I cannot accept that the matters are closed and the discussion ended.

Tony Flannery CSsR'